Media and the Myth of the Pristine Night

Media and the Myth of the Pristine Night

Dwayne Avery

ANTHEM PRESS

Anthem Press
An imprint of Wimbledon Publishing Company
www.anthempress.com

This edition first published in UK and USA 2026
by ANTHEM PRESS
75–76 Blackfriars Road, London SE1 8HA, UK
or PO Box 9779, London SW19 7ZG, UK
and
244 Madison Ave #116, New York, NY 10016, USA

First published in the UK and USA by Anthem Press in 2025

British Library Cataloguing-in-Publication Data
A catalogue record for this book is available from the British Library.

Library of Congress Cataloging-in-Publication Data: 2026941619

ISBN-13: 978-1-80136-055-5 (Pbk)
ISBN-10: 1-80136-055-3 (Pbk)

Cover credit: Dwayne Avery

This title is also available as an eBook.

CONTENTS

LIST OF FIGURES

INTRODUCTION

The Rise of the "Night Mayor"

In June 2024, Canada's capital city, Ottawa, appointed Mathieu Grondin as its first nightlife commissioner. The position, often called a "night mayor," reflects the growing importance of cities to create a robust and diverse nighttime economy. Indeed, Ottawa's decision to create a new branch of municipal government just to shed its image as a bureaucratic place that doesn't know how to have fun (MacDiarind, 2024) is emblematic of a global trend in urban governance that recognizes the urban night as a vital part of city life, deserving its own strategic policies and development. To further support Grondin's efforts, the city even appointed a "nightlife council," a body tasked with the goal of enhancing the positive activities that take place after the workday ends. Like other nighttime councils, the group hopes to shape and grow the city's nightlife while recognizing the new challenges (noise complaints, crime, public intoxication, light pollution, etc.) associated with ramping up the urban night's leisure activities.

While Ottawa is the latest in a growing list of North American cities that have night mayors, the idea that the urban night offers opportunities and challenges that differ from those of the day and, therefore, require special nocturnal advocates is far from new. In the 1970s, the late Dutch poet Jules Deelder gained such an influential role in the cultural life of Rotterdam that he was nicknamed the "night mayor" of the city. In 2014, Amsterdam became the first city to formally institutionalize the role and created a series of independent organizations that use strategic management, advocacy, mediation, and diversity promotion (Petrovics and Seijas) to support the urban night. As appointed institutions working alongside elected officials, these nocturnal advocates demonstrate how the management of contemporary cities requires new models of governance that understand the night's unique attributes and growth potential.

Following Amsterdam's lead, other major European cities, including London, Berlin, and Paris, have adopted similar positions. The trend has spread rapidly, with over eighty cities currently having night mayors or similar roles. This widespread adoption highlights not only the growing importance of nighttime economies for generating urban wealth and investment opportunities but also a paradigm shift in how city officials perceive darkness. For most of human history, the night was understood through a traditional framework that saw it as a time of sleep and rest, a period of dormancy separated from the sustained productivity of the day. However, with the rise of the 24-hour city and global competition for investment dollars, urban officials recognize the night's economic potential and the need for a more nuanced approach to managing the city that envisions nighttime as a key to urban growth. According to the influential placemaking and marketing agency, *Toposophy*, "The night economy is not just a significant contributor to urban economies; its resilience through challenging times underscores its potential for growth. With cities like [...] New York and Sydney demonstrating its substantial role in GDP and employment, the sector presents untapped opportunities for economic expansion" (Toposophy).

In a neoliberal system that seeks to extract as much economic value from social life, the night mayor trend can be understood as the mechanism by which the night, long thought to be the last bastion of defense against capital (Crary) is forced to conform to the rhythms of capitalism. This economic reading, however, fails to acknowledge a fair, great social shift in reassessing the cultural value of darkness. Urban darkness, once perceived as a source of fear or danger, is now the source of a wide variety of new cultural opportunities and power dynamics. From the use of light shows to bolster the city's entertainment districts to the creation of underground "youth scenes" that thrive in peripheral parts of the city, the interplay of darkness and light is a crucial part of the city's political identity. As Will Straw (2018) writes, [...] "the politics of the night are, in a variety of ways, a sensory politics." Like the night mayor trend, the idea that the night offers sensory capacities that are deeply political is not unprecedented. The historian Bryan Palmer has argued that the night has long held political significance as a space where subversive activities can evade scrutiny. From clandestine meetings and secret plots to covert acts of resistance and illicit practices, the night has proven to be a space-time dedicated to political upheaval. Similarly, in his influential examination of the frontier qualities of the night, Murray Melbin writes that the night's political power emerges from its function as a refuge, allowing minorities space to find like-minded outcasts and gain restorative strength in marginalized communities that thrive in the cloak of darkness.

In this book, I build on the observation that darkness is not simply a passive backdrop to social activity, but a sensory force that actively shapes and influences power relations, social inequalities, and political struggles. However, where my work differs from other night studies scholars resides in my argument that the urban night not only fosters progressive engagements with darkness but regressive imaginings that retreat from the material realities of the contemporary city. That is, while the rise of urban mayors signals the growing need to politicize the urban night, many dark-sky advocates depoliticize darkness by promoting and proselytizing the values of the pristine and untouched. Walter Benjamin's seemingly paradoxical idea that the desire to retreat from modern life works in tandem with modernity is a crucial aspect of my approach to understanding the myth of pristine darkness. Just as Benjamin suggests that various forms of nostalgia and traditionalism are not simply alternatives to modernity but are, in fact, deeply intertwined with the very forces they attempt to escape, the idea of retreating to a pristine, untouched night sky is the byproduct of a highly electrified, neoliberal world that has colonized the night.

To support this claim, *Media and the Myth of the Pristine Night* provides a critical and comprehensive account of the mediation of pristine darkness. Analyzing a wide range of contemporary media, from astrophotography, tourist advertisements, and social media to editing software, art installations, and nature documentaries, the book focuses on two competing and irreconcilable cultures of darkness. On the one hand, many forms of mass media contribute to a "preservation" ideology based on the Western myth of "wilderness." Relying on the classic urban/rural binary, this culture of darkness imagines the night as a pristine, ancient inheritance, a distant and remote frontier free from the ills of human technology. On the other hand, other media genres challenge this preservationist depiction of darkness, demonstrating that does not retreat from modern, urban life but is an extension of the urban-technological. Using a hybrid view of the night, I contend that pristine darkness serves as a cultural technology that erases the messy connections between the rural and the urban. Not only does the preservationist view of pristine darkness privilege "natural" darkness over other sustainable forms of gloom, but its endorsement of the frontier myth represents a flight from history, a rhetorical strategy that may prevent the night's protection.

Thus, while urban mayors and other advocacy groups continue to advance a politics of the night that focuses on urban policy and governance, equally important are the representational media that shape and define a wide variety of nocturnal geographies. As I hope to show, although the pristine night may not be on the radar of many night mayors, this form of darkness is connected to urban systems in complicated ways and requires an interdisciplinary approach that move us beyond the urban.

Night Studies

Although scholars have always taken an interest in the cultural and social life of the night, over the past decade, an unprecedented body of interdisciplinary research has emerged that considers how the night shapes human behavior, urban space, and cultural practices. From studies on the ecological impacts of urban light pollution and the dire health effects of working the "night shift" to studies into tourists' perceptions of the night and urban youth cultures, scholars in the burgeoning field of night studies continue to unpack the extensive ways the night shapes the contours of life. Merging insights from various disciplines, from urban design, philosophy, and economics to biology, anthropology, and media studies (Gwiazdzinski, 2016; van Liempt et al., 2015), night studies coalesce around what Craig Koslofsky (2011) calls the nocturnalization thesis, the observation that daytime activities, such as leisure time, have been pushed further into the night over the past two centuries. At the apex of this nocturnalization process is the emergence of the 24/7 city, a place of colonial expansionism, whereby widespread electrical illumination recalibrates the cosmological frontier between night and day, such that the capitalist rhythms of the day increasingly colonize the night (Crary, 2013).

Historically, the night has been perceived as a shapeless time of activity, a place of reprieve, overshadowed by the day's productive rhythms (Schlör, 1998). However, recent historical research reveals that nighttime has always been composed of a vibrant tapestry of activities. In this eclectic space–time, work, leisure, and social life intertwine in unique ways, challenging the notion of nocturnal passivity and illuminating the night as a dynamic space teeming with life. For example, in *Evening's Empire: A History of the Night in Early Modern Europe* (2011), Koslofsky traces the historical and cultural evolution of nighttime practices in Europe. While nighttime was perceived as a time of fear and menacing dangers in Medieval Europe, during the early modern period, night shifted to become a site of sociopolitical and cultural significance. As more people began to venture outside of their homes after dark, a new nightlife began to take shape, with many leisure activities, such as dining out and going to the theatre, being pushed further into the night. As Koslofsky observes,

> Nocturnalization touched all aspects of early modern culture [...] At royal courts and in cities, nocturnalization unfolded (and is most visible to scholars) in the years after 1650, when mealtimes, the closing schedules of city gates, the beginning of theatrical performances and balls, and closing times of taverns all moved several hours later. In the same years, the nonalcoholic beverages chocolate, coffee, and tea surged in popularity—and coffeehouses, notorious for their late hours, appeared in all European cities by 1700. Of all these developments, the swift rise of public street lighting is the most salient: in 1660, no European city had permanently illuminated its streets, but by 1700 consistent and reliable street lighting had been established in Amsterdam, Paris, Turin,

> London, and Copenhagen, and across the Holy Roman Empire from Hamburg to Vienna. Fear of the night was now mingled with improved conditions for labor and leisure as the emerging modern night began to show its characteristic ambivalence.

Joachim Schlör's historical research into the nightlife of late modernity paints a similar story. In *Nights in the Big City,* Schlör examines the transformation of urban nightlife in Paris, Berlin, and London between 1840 and 1930. For Schlör, the key to the rise of new forms of nocturnal sociability was the emergence of the "illuminated night," the idea that it was the widespread adoption of gas and electric lighting that altered the perception and experience of the night in these major cities. Not only did the illuminated night provide ample sources of nighttime leisure and entertainment, such as late-night cafés, theatres, and music halls, but the streets themselves became lively spaces for strolling and socializing under the glow of streetlight. With this increase in nocturnal socialization came both exciting opportunities for exploring different illicit activities and the subsequent perceived need for increased forms of urban surveillance. The anonymity of the night provided fertile ground for the development of subcultures and alternative lifestyles. Prostitution, crime, and other illicit activities flourished under the cover of darkness, enhancing the anxieties and fascinations surrounding the nocturnal city.

Although much recent historical work on the night has altered our understanding of previous experiences with darkness, it is the foundational work of the sociologist Murray Melbin that has illuminated our understanding of contemporary experiences with nighttime. In *Night as Frontier: Colonizing the World After Dark*, Melbin (1987) draws a compelling analogy between the historical westward expansion across land frontiers and the modern "colonization" of the night to show how the night has been rapidly colonized for work, leisure, and urban development. As urban societies move toward creating a 24/7 society, people encounter a new nocturnal frontier with its own set of challenges, opportunities, and social dynamics. Melbin supports his argument by identifying similarities between nighttime activities and life on traditional frontiers. Just as early settlers perceived the West as a vast, unpopulated space, according to Melbin, those who venture into the night encounter a world with fewer people, allowing for a sense of freedom and anonymity. Likewise, with fewer authorities and social constraints, nighttime offers greater individual autonomy and opportunities for self-expression. Finally, like frontiers, the night fosters innovation and experimentation, leading to the development of new social structures and subcultures.

Although Melbin's work was carried out at a time when the so-called 24/7 society was not fully developed and thus oversimplifies and romanticizes some aspects of the frontier mythology associated with the night, his work has laid the foundation for a wide range of contemporary inquiries into the meaning of the urban night. The British geographers Tim Edensor and Nick Dunn, for example, have provided rich and often personal understandings of the night's sensory and aesthetic experiences. In *From Light to Dark: Daylight, Illumination, and Gloom*, Edensor (2017) provides a fascinating exploration of the multifaceted ways humans interact with light and darkness in their urban environments. Going beyond the simple dichotomy of day and night, Edensor delves into the nuances of daylight, artificial illumination, and varying degrees of darkness, revealing their profound impact on human perception, emotions, and social interactions. One of the most notable aspects of Edensor's research is that under some conditions, the cloak of darkness can enhance feelings of social security and intimacy. While urban places at night have long been stigmatized as places of criminality and other risks, Edensor demonstrates that darkness can facilitate prosocial connections that work to dislodge many of the pejorative qualities associated with the night.

Similarly, Nick Dunn's *Dark Matters: A Manifesto for the Nocturnal City* (2016) advocates for embracing darkness as an integral part of urban life, challenging the pervasive view that a safe and reliable city is one dependent on excessive illumination. Specifically, Dunn explores the history of night walking and its association with miscreants and transgressors. While mainstream media has turned these experiences into anxieties about the urban night, Dunn highlights the potential for positive experiences in the urban landscape after dark. Walking alone in the dark can not only help one gain distance from the pervasive "always on" mentality of 24/7 capitalism, but it can lead to bursts of creativity and new, unexpected relationships with the city and its inhabitants. As Dunn writes:

> Walking in cities at night, therefore, enables us to sense, connect and think with the city around us. We are able to give things our undivided attention, a welcome respite from the ongoing erosion and subdivision of our time and sense of belonging in the world. Deliberately moving out of the glare and stare of our commoditized and highly structured daily routines and into the rich shadows and patina of our cities at night may be one of the few truly beautiful and sublime practices available to us. Far from being dead hours, for the wakeful, the night affords investigation and liberation. It is an essential part of living: an important counterpoint to responsibilities assumed in the daytime.

Together, these scholars (along with many others) have helped establish night studies as a vibrant and growing field of inquiry. This work not only challenges traditional assumptions about the night, revealing its complexities and the many ways light and dark shape urban life, but it demonstrates that as cities increasingly embrace the 24-hour model, night studies will play a crucial role in informing urban planning, policy-making, and our understanding of the urban experience.

Media and the Urban Night

Once shrouded in mystery and associated primarily with sleep and seclusion, the urban night has undergone a dramatic transformation in recent times. While this shift is inextricably linked to various evolutionary forces, from the widespread adoption of artificial lighting to the rise of the tourist city, the mass media have also played a pivotal role in shaping perceptions about cities after dark. One of the most significant ways in which the mass media have impacted the urban night is through exploratory narratives where the nocturnal city serves as a unique place of discovery (Straw, 2015). "The night, in this mode," Straw writes, "is the time/space of a journey, typically organized as a series of encounters with people and places." While exploratory narratives set around the urban night have undoubtedly evolved over time, one of the most common stories is the idea that the night is a dangerous, exotic, and forbidden place, which leads innocent people astray. In early twentieth-century cinema, for example, films like Fritz Lang's *Metropolis* (1927) depicted the night as a place of alienation and intrigue, where the struggles of the working classes were counterposed to the new leisure activities and sensory delights sought after by the upper classes. Such media representations often reinforced dualistic perceptions of the night as both liberating and dangerous. Likewise, noir films of the mid-twentieth century, with their dimly lit streets and morally ambiguous characters, further cemented the night as a site of mystery and transgression, shaping cultural imaginations of urban life after dark. Cultural narratives of the urban night are also evident in journalism and photography. The works of Weegee, a New York City photojournalist of the 1930s and 1940s, captured the gritty realities of crime and nightlife, providing visceral documentation of the night's vibrancy and violence. These visual and textual narratives did more than document the realities of the night; they shaped public perceptions of the urban night, influencing policies and behaviors.

Despite growing concerns over the exotic dangers of cities at night, throughout the nineteenth century, the urban night maintained a strong allure. As many urban historians have documented, the shadowy and sinister image of the city coincided with an obverse world of playful and dazzling electric lighting. If film noir imagined the night as a place of darkened alleyways and imperceptible street-corners, urban advertisers gave the city a vibrant glow, inviting people to venture out to bathe in the excessively bright, vibrant, and visually striking advertisements that illuminated the city. The proliferation of illuminated billboards, signage, and architecture was just some of the many ways modern lighting transformed the visual landscape of cities after dark. In *Weimar Surfaces: Urban Visual Culture in 1920s Germany*, Janet Ward (2001) notes how the cities' electrification dramatically altered the night's experience. Streets, buildings, and public spaces were bathed in artificial light, creating a dazzling spectacle that transformed the urban landscape. New approaches to urban advertising were incredibly transformative, as the combination of urban lighting and impressive advertisements created a nighttime aesthetic that celebrated the frenzied, fast-paced tempos of modern life. As Ward observes:

> By the mid-1920s, when the experiential focus of electric light had become more settled as a transformer of the urban context, its presence was a fixture of more coolly ironic, New Objectively functional representations [...] New Objective ways of understanding electricity's presence were used with great success in advertising itself. As a tourism poster of 1925 announced, Berlin wanted to "see you" on its streets, like the ones shown spinning around the Kaiser Wilhelm Memorial Church—so that the city could behold itself in its proconsumer scenes of electric spectacle. Paris's attempted transformation out of its nineteenth-century image was marked by the Eiffel Tower's electric advertisement for Citroen—a vertically descending column with the company name alternating with a pattern of light—the largest in the world during the 1920s, and likened in its effect to the monumental way in which Niagara Falls was enhanced electrically by night.

Another way the mass media impacted the urban night is by altering human perceptions of time. With the advent of twenty-four-hour news cycles, continuous radio and television broadcasting, and the ubiquitous internet, the rhythmic availability of the mass media has helped shape and define society's experience of day and night. Writing about the role the media play in structuring the rhythms of the twenty-four-hour cycle, Will Straw (2015) notes, "Major media of the 20th centuries, from radio through television, participate in what Paddy Scannell (1986) and others have called the 'flow' of media content throughout the 24-hour cycle. This flow may produce a sense of relatively undifferentiated time and mark the differences between day and night in only minor ways. Conversely, through the ways in which they appear, disappear or change their programming over the course of a day, media may endow different parts of the 24-hour cycle with distinct identities."

According to Straw, the ability of the media to endow different parts of the twenty-four-hour cycle with distinct identities has everything to do with the combination of media content and the time of media consumption. For example, radio has long played a significant role in shaping urbanites' experiences with the flow of time: whereas early morning radio often preps workers for their morning commute through upbeat music, late night music is set apart by edgier songs and cultural experimentation. Similarly, the scheduling of television broadcasts has helped shape cultural experiences and expectations about the meaning of the night. Whereas prime-time television features lavish and expensive productions that garner the largest audiences and are associated with the new and contemporary, late-night television, which is cheap to produce and often features re-runs, has long been a way television has celebrated the legacies of the cultural past.

With the arrival of "always on" digital media, it is sometimes perceived that the media's ability to organize the temporal rhythms of night and day is waning. Can there be a nighttime internet or nocturnal social media when the proliferation of digital media and streaming services makes everything available at all times of the day? In a recent article for *The Atlantic*, media studies scholar Ian Bogost explores this always-on connectivity in terms of the prolific rise of the so-called "dark mode," a display setting that flips the traditional color scheme of an interface, presenting content with light-colored text and UI elements on a dark background. Bogost traces the meteoric rise of this aesthetic choice to early computer coders who used this inverse style of presenting digital information to reduce the visual strain of working in over-illuminated office buildings. According to Bogost, since we now spend most of our time looking at the ever-pervasive mobile screen, the need for "night" or "dark" modes represents a collective desire for a retreat into a space free from the ubiquity of media virtuality.

Although Bogost doesn't make any explicit connections between night modes and actual darkness, the dark mode trend, I think, speaks to a social desire for an earlier time when the well-organized machinery of the media produced stable and recognizable rituals of consumption that helped organize the pulse and flows of the transition from day to night. Luckily, it seems that we are seeing some evidence that social media platforms, online forums, and mobile applications are creating distinct urban spaces that allow for social interaction and community building after dark. Along with providing new formats for the representation of urban life, these digital platforms have facilitated new ways to organize cultural events, share information, and form nocturnal communities, contributing to a more vibrant and interconnected urban night. Indeed, in the digital age, social media platforms like Instagram and TikTok may even amplify our exposure to the unique qualities of the urban night, turning nightlife experiences into performative spaces for influencer cultures. Bars, clubs, and cultural events are increasingly seen as curated experiences meant for documentation and sharing, redefining the night through the lens of digital consumption.

It remains to be seen if this desire will lead to the more distinct identities created by earlier forms of mass media. But what is certain is that the media and the urban night are deeply intertwined, with media shaping how the night is experienced, understood, and valued. From cultural narratives in film and literature to digital technologies' transformative impact, media reflects and constructs the urban night. However, this relationship is not without its tensions, as issues of representation, commodification, and surveillance complicate how nocturnal spaces are mediated. As cities continue to evolve, the study of media and the urban night offers critical insights into how technology and culture intersect in the ever-changing landscape of the nocturnal world.

Moving Beyond the Urban Night

Although the burgeoning field of night studies has significantly altered our understanding of the night, especially by overcoming the myth that night is a time of passivity, as a whole, research into the night maintains several oversights and biases. The most notable is the way the night has become interchangeable with the *urban* night; other nocturnal geographies, like the pristine night, the rural night, or the suburban night, have failed to gain the same kind of traction as the urban night. The reasons behind this preference for urbanity are not difficult to decipher. Since the rise of the so-called "network city," the idea that modern power is facilitated through a network of urban centers, the city has become synonymous with globalization. In his influential book, *The Informational City*, Manual Castells (1992), for example, argues that cities have become central nodes in the global network of information flows. In the network age, cities are spaces where information is produced, processed, and disseminated, driving economic growth and social change. Likewise, as a key agent of globalization, the informational city is characterized less by its physicality, like the nation-state, than by its interconnectedness with other cities and regions worldwide. The "space of flows" is the concept Castells uses to describe the new spatial logic of the informational society. In a global order dominated by networks, the space of flows is responsible for rapidly moving people, capital, and information between several key urban zones of influence.

Along with the idea of the network society, the "creative city" paradigm has also raised the status of the city, referring to it as the paradigmatic place for creative innovation. Emerging in the late twentieth century as a response to economic restructuring and the rise of the knowledge economy, the creative city paradigm explores how cities can foster creativity and innovation to drive economic growth, social inclusion, and urban regeneration. In his influential book *The Creative City*, Charles Landry (2012) emphasizes how cities cultivate a "creative climate" through investments in cultural infrastructure, human capital, and public spaces that encourage interaction and innovation. Similarly, Richard Florida's (2017; 2019) work on the creative classes, the idea that the economic engine of modern capitalism can be found in the three T's (technology, talent, and tolerance), also calls attention to the city's unique ability to foster vibrant cultural scenes, diverse communities, and a high quality of life. Not only are creative cities responsible for the growth of knowledge-based economies, but they concentrate talent in what Florida calls superstar cities, a select group of metropolitan areas that have become dominant economic and cultural hubs in the global economy.

Given how some urban geographers continue to advance the city through what Robert Beauregard (2003) calls an urban boosterism based on superlatives, it's not surprising that studies of the night tend to focus on urban issues such as nightlife, cultural scenes, safety, and light pollution. Unfortunately, this urban bias has led to an incomplete understanding of the night. By focusing primarily on urban environments, the field of night studies misses out on crucial insights into other important nocturnal geographies. To address this bias, this book explores how the pervasive interest in the urban night, mostly readily symbolized by the night mayor, has given shape to a longing for other kinds of nocturnal geographies. Specifically, I argue that the relentless drive to maximize the economic potential of the urban night, through intensified illumination has ironically fueled nostalgic movements yearning for the pristine tranquility of "true" darkness. I call this form of darkness the myth of the pristine night. To explore this myth, I turn to the powerful role media play in shaping perceptions of darkness. Exploring a variety of diverse media forms, ranging from breathtaking astrophotography and evocative tourist posters promoting "dark sky" destinations, to innovative software designed to measure and combat light pollution, and compelling nature documentaries showcasing nocturnal ecosystems, it will become clear that the myth of the pristine night is pervasive and deeply ingrained in contemporary consciousness. These media, while often celebrating the beauty and ecological importance of darkness, simultaneously highlight its increasing scarcity, further fueling a nostalgic longing for a natural nocturnal environment.

The Myth of Pristine Darkness

In his seminal work, *Mythologies*, Roland Barthes describes myth as a second-order semiological system. Myths take already existing signs (the Milky Way) and turn them into a new, broader system of cultural meaning (pristine darkness is the proper way to experience the night sky). Essentially, myth naturalizes historical and cultural messages, making contingent social constructs appear as universal, self-evident truths. It empties the original sign of its complexity and fills it with a new, often ideological, meaning that serves the dominant culture. Myths don't necessarily lie, but rather distort and simplifies reality to promote a particular worldview.

Barthes' ideas on mythmaking are helpful for understanding how advanced technological societies often understand nature through a chain of signifiers that translates individual signs, such as forests, rivers, or darkness, into a connotative system that envisions nature's beauty as a direct product of its purity. Here, purity and pristineness maintain a moral quality, wherein nature is considered more real and genuine because it is free from human involvement. Finally, as a resource uncontaminated by human civilization, pure nature is invested with considerable symbolic value, as it is often considered a place of escape or spiritual renewal. By presenting nature as pristine, myths often naturalize a particular historical moment, transforming a specific, idealized past into a rarified version of reality, ignoring the dynamic and ever-changing nature of ecosystems and the long history of human interaction with them. Myths, in this way, can de-politicize reality, obscuring the historical and ongoing impacts of human actions and the social and political dimensions of environmental degradation.

Like Barthes' ideas on myth, Claude Lévi-Strauss's structuralism, while not directly focused on environmental issues, also offers a powerful framework for understanding how we perceive and conceptualize "pristine nature." His work, particularly on mythology and binary systems, emphasizes the underlying structures of human thought that shape cultural categories and understandings of the world. For Lévi-Strauss, myths aren't just stories but structured systems of meaning that address fundamental contradictions within a culture. The idea of "pristine nature" can function as a kind of modern myth which embodies certain values (purity, authenticity, escape) that helps society negotiate its relationship with the environment. For example, the myth of pristine darkness might resolve the tension between the social desire for technological progress and a nostalgia for a perceived natural past free from light pollution. Furthermore, Lévi-Strauss argued that human thought operates through fundamental binary oppositions (e.g., raw/cooked, nature/culture, wild/domesticated). From this view, the concept of "pristine darkness" gains its meaning in opposition to "culture" or the "technological." By examining this binary, it becomes apparent that the idea of untouched wilderness or pristine darkness is constructed as something separate and distinct from human society.

As I will argue throughout this book, the notion of a pristine night sky, untouched by human influence, is a nostalgic fallacy. While earlier societies undoubtedly experienced nights darker than ours, the concept of pristine darkness devoid of any alteration ignores the historical interplay between humanity and the night. From the first campfires to the ubiquitous glow of modern cities, technology has continuously reshaped our perception of darkness. As Jane Brox shows, one of the earliest and most significant changes to the night sky occurred with the control of fire. While providing warmth and safety, fire also cast the first artificial light into the night, pushing back the boundaries of darkness and altering nocturnal animal behavior. The invention of the candle and, later, the gas lamp further intensified this effect, bringing artificial illumination to streets and homes, albeit on a limited scale. This localized light pollution, though less pervasive than today's, still disrupted the natural rhythms of darkness (Brox, 2010).

The most radical shift to the experience of darkness began with the advent of electricity and the incandescent light bulb. Suddenly, affordable and readily available light allowed for unprecedented illumination of cities and towns. This marked the beginning of widespread light pollution, with its detrimental effects on astronomy, wildlife, and even human health (Longcore and Rich, 2013; Zallen, 2019). The rise of urbanization further exacerbated the issue, as sprawling cities became beacons of artificial light, drowning out the stars and disrupting ecosystems. The twentieth century saw an explosion of technologies that further eroded the darkness of night. Neon signs, streetlights, and floodlights became ubiquitous, creating a constant, ambient glow in urban areas. The development of motor vehicles with powerful headlights added another layer of nocturnal illumination, extending the reach of artificial light far beyond city limits (Isenstadt).

In recent decades, the rise of digital technology has introduced new forms of light pollution. LED screens, ubiquitous in smartphones, billboards, and buildings, emit bright, blue-rich light that is particularly disruptive to circadian rhythms and nocturnal wildlife (Caraveo, 2021). The proliferation of communication towers and satellites has also added to the skyglow, casting an ever-present veil over even the most remote locations. Even seemingly benign technologies contribute to the problem. In rural areas, greenhouses, designed to extend the growing season, often leak light into the night sky, creating eerie beacons of light visible for miles. Oil and gas flares, a byproduct of fossil fuel extraction in rural areas, also illuminate vast swathes of land, transforming the night into an industrial landscape.

Although light pollution represents a major ecological issue, the problem with many efforts to conserve darkness is that in order to recover the awe-inspiring and wonderous experience of viewing the pristine night, we must return to an earlier period of human history, one free from the moral destitution of artificial light. For example, in his work, *The End of the Night*, Paul Bogard (2014) incessantly differentiates between the "real" night, which is associated with the purity of the past, and the "artificial" night, a fake form of darkness that is associated with urban simulation and inauthenticity. Writing about New York, Bogard claims that "it no longer feels like night. And by that I mean it no longer feels dark. In fact, at least in terms of darkness, 'real night,' no longer exists in New York or in Las Vegas, or in hundreds of cities across the world."

Bogard is not the only one who uses the rhetoric of the pristine night to promote the cultural value of darkness. Many of the most recognizable dark-sky preservation organizations, such as the International Dark-Sky Association (IDA) and the British Astronomical Association, often rely on the myth of the pristine night, pitting the pristine nature of rural darkness against the artifice of cities. The IDA, for instance, is a non-profit organization with a mission to preserve and protect the nighttime environment and the cultural heritage of dark skies through environmentally responsible outdoor lighting. As the leading authority combating light pollution worldwide, the IDA has considerable power to define not only what light pollution is but also the cultural, scientific, and aesthetic value of darkness. No doubt, the IDA is a remarkable organization. It has made significant strides to educate the public about the negative impacts of light pollution, including its effects on human health, wildlife, and the environment. On a practical level, they have been great in promoting responsible lighting, advocating for the use of outdoor lighting that is efficient, targeted, and minimizes glare and skyglow. They also provide resources and guidelines for individuals, businesses, and policymakers on implementing dark-sky friendly lighting practices.

Despite these international efforts to preserve darkness, the IDA often relies on several rhetorical myths that can potentially undermine its practical approach to fighting light pollution. For example, one of the IDA's most well-known initiatives is its Dark Sky Places Program: the IDA designates locations worldwide as International Dark Sky Places, recognizing their commitment to preserving dark skies. These places include parks, communities, and reserves that meet strict criteria for lighting and public education. While this program incentivizes communities to take action and provides models for others to follow, the promotional materials for these Dark-Sky reserves often depend on modern forms of astronomical tourism that highlight the tension and challenges of combating modern environmental problems through rustic and overtly romantic images of the rural heartland. Along with the many contradictions associated with ecotourism, such as the industry's dependence on urban trends in cultural consumption or the expectation of urban infrastructure and amenities (hotels, spas, and so on), the promotion of Dark-Sky reserves often depends on various outdated and nostalgic images of "wild" nature. Indeed, since most Dark-Sky parks are located in pre-existing nature parks that have been built around the desire for untainted nature, free from the ills of modern urbanization, the desire for the pristine starry night falls into many of the same rhetorical pitfalls of thinking about nature as something existing outside human civilization.

In his work on the British Astronomical Association's Campaign for Dark Skies (CfDS), Oliver Dunnet notes a similar trend: like Bogard, the CfDS offers a moral account of light pollution through a standard rhetorical coupling. Whereas light pollution is associated with the spread of urbanization, which the group portrays as an encroaching force that threatens the natural darkness of rural areas, pristine darkness is imagined as a spiritual resource that evokes the astronomical sublime. While the campaign engages with the lighting industry to encourage the adoption of more efficient technologies and practices, its fight against light pollution ends up promoting a moral dichotomy that undervalues and undermines urban societies. Drawing on childhood memories of stargazing and representations of ancient landscapes like Stonehenge under pristine night, the CfDS' campaign not only alienates urban populations by treating them as a problem but fosters an unrealistic expectation of what the starry night should look like and evoke.

At the heart of this binary distinction (real vs. artificial darkness) is a pervasive anti-urban sentiment that continues to wreak havoc on how we treat social and ecological issues. In *Americans Against the City: Anti-Urbanism in the Twentieth Century,* Steven Conn (2014) provides a thought-provoking analysis of the persistent anti-urbanism that has shaped American society and its physical landscape. Conn argues that this anti-urban impulse has roots in nineteenth-century romantic movements and has manifested in various forms throughout the twentieth century, influencing everything from suburbanization and urban renewal to the rise of the New Right. For Conn, anti-urbanism is intertwined with a yearning for an idealized past rooted in agrarianism and small-town life. For example, during the inter-war period, the public became fascinated by various "back to the land" and homesteading campaigns that sought to protect the moral worth of the private individual against the vices of urban modernity. As Conn writes: "During those same years, Americans who wanted to leave the city, and de-centralize [...] needed examples of an alternative to urban America. They "discovered" one such alternative in the American "folk"—people whose patterns of living has not been corrupted by urban and industrial America, and who could serve as a model for a de-urbanized future."

To avoid these moral retreats into agrarian fantasies and understand the complex relationships between technology, humanity, and the natural world, it is vital to recognize the myths associated with the pristine and pure. Thus, in my cultural assessment of darkness, I aim to demonstrate that the pristine night is fraught with contradictions that seek to conceal the technological alterations of the night sky and its connection to urban cultures. In the remainder of this section, I outline three of the key contradictions associated with the myth of the pristine night: these include dark sky tourism, technological mediation, and network connectivity.

Tourism: The Marketed Rural Retreat and Its Urban Roots

Like other forms of ecotourism, the pristine night fuels the tourist industry, attracting urban dwellers seeking respite from the perceived ills of city life. For example, The International Dark Sky Association strategically harnesses the allure of pristine night skies to champion dark sky preservation by certifying locations renowned for their minimal light pollution as International Dark Sky Places. This certification acts as a powerful draw for astro-tourists, individuals eager to experience the cosmos in its natural splendor, often leading to significant increases in visitation and providing a tangible economic incentive for communities and protected areas to prioritize dark sky protection. The IDA actively promotes these certified havens, guiding travellers to these exceptional viewing sites and simultaneously raising awareness about the detrimental effects of light pollution. By underscoring the economic advantages of astro-tourism, such as increased revenue generation, extended tourism seasons, and job creation, the IDA encourages destinations to recognize their dark skies as unique and valuable assets. Furthermore, the influx of tourists to these areas creates opportunities for education on responsible lighting practices and the broader importance of the natural night, often facilitated through specialized visitor experiences, such as stargazing tours and astronomy programs.

While this desire for rustic wonder can provide tourists with sublime experiences, organizations like the IDA often employ rhetorical strategies that obscure and downplay the urban infrastructure that makes such experiences possible. That is, while seemingly offering an escape, astro-tourism relies on urban consumption patterns that actively transform rural landscapes to cater to urban desires. This paradox, the idea that urban consumption and infrastructure produce rural forms of escape, has been explored by Richard Grusin, whose work on the national park movement in the US demonstrates that "wild" and "pristine" nature is neither natural nor exists outside of culture, but is a direct product of the tourist industry. In *Culture, Technology, and the Creation of America's National Parks*, Grusin argues that the burgeoning tourism industry in the late nineteenth century was not merely a consequence of the parks' establishment, but rather an integral force in their creation and the shaping of their meaning. For example, the increasing accessibility of these landscapes resulted from the development of transportation networks, such as railroads. Likewise, tourist media, such as posters and advertisements, aligned with the aesthetic sensibilities of the time and contributed to the idea that these places were national treasures worthy of preservation for public enjoyment. Finally, the immense economic potential for tourism-driven development provided a compelling argument for establishing national parks. Proponents could point to the revenue generated by hotels, transportation, and other tourist-related industries. This economic incentive often swayed political decisions and local interests in favor of park designation. Through these contributing factors, Grusin sees tourism as a crucial "technology"—a system of practices, infrastructure, and representations—that actively shapes the cultural understanding and value attributed to "pristine" landscapes.

According to Luc Gwiazdzinski and Will Straw the tension between the touristic desire to preserve the "ancestral qualities of the pristine starry night" and the simultaneous push to inject urban forms of sociability into these same rural spaces to attract economic development is evident in what they call the "mountain night." Whereas mountains are often perceived as uninhabitable frontiers, in recent years, the expansion of tourism and leisure activities into remote regions has led to a variety of transformative processes. As they write:

> In these mountain territories that are not spared by the extension of the domain of day, the night is a resource now exploited by many actors: landscapes transformed by light, illuminated ski slopes, new leisure offers, nocturnal operation of sports and tourist facilities, new uses, new representations, new identities and nocturnal tourism marketing. Better still, this conquest of the night and the mountains acts as a double indicator of the tensions and paradoxes that run through our societies in terms of sustainable development. Mountain nights are wonderful spaces-times for investigation, creativity and experimentation that force us to rethink our ways of living and dwelling as a way of knowing the world and a type of emotional relationships far from an abstract or technocratic approach to space.

For Gwiazdzinski and Straw, the "mountain night" is a hybrid experience that positions the night at crossroads: on the one hand, many tourist developers look to transform rural mountain regions through urban experiences, especially by opening the pristine night to the transgressive forms of sociability that have emerged out of urban nightlife. On the other hand, many activists wish to preserve the ancestral qualities of the pristine starry night, safeguarding the night from all the so-called ills associated with urban decadence. As they write:

> Here, the night is to be valued, not only as an "ancient" resource in danger of disappearing, but as an antidote to several ills of technological modernity: the psychophysical effects of light pollution on multiple species, the economic and environmental costs of artificial illumination, and the loss of any human connection with the supposedly natural cycles of night and day, darkness and light, work and rest. These well-known "battles" in the heart of cities are also located in the mountains and other territories considered "peripheral" to urban life. From the Pyrenees to Java, we are witnessing a movement of patrimonialization of the night similar to that which has affected little-anthropized environments (forests, etc.) and which has often led to protective measures. Here too, we find this clash between the defenders of a primordial experience of the celestial night and those for whom the "natural" space of the mountain (or the desert or the sub-oceanic space) offers opportunities for new forms of experimentation and spectacularization intended to attract tourists and other forces and actors of economic development.

Technology: Illuminating the Pristine Night with Urban Innovations

The myth of the pristine night often imagines darkness as untouched by technological advancements. However, this ignores the pervasive influence of technology in shaping contemporary rural life and its nocturnal experiences. From the blue glow of smartphones illuminating faces in remote areas to the satellite internet connecting isolated communities to the global network, technology is deeply embedded in the pristine night. While proponents of pure darkness lament light pollution as an "ill of technological modernity," the very technologies they utilize for stargazing—smartphone apps, online sky maps, digital cameras—are products of urban technological innovation. According to Darin Barney and Laticia Chapman, this approach to remote and wild places is a consistent ideological fallacy that fails to understand the technological breakthroughs and practices that exist outside urban centers. As Laticia Chapman writes, "Emptiness is a projection that permits us to see rural places as lacking and in need of intervention, often in the form of grand plans that imply the sweeping question "what could we do here?" But one could also ask the question "what is happening here?" inviting rural infrastructure, technology, practices, histories, and ideas to disclose themselves in their fullness."

Contrary to conventional wisdom, rural areas do not lag behind their urban counterparts in terms of innovative uses of modern technology, but at times lead the way. As Barney writes, "In the turn from work to flow, industrial agriculture and the rural locations in which it occurs, especially those with colonial histories, are paradigmatic, not outlying—leading, not lagging, central, not peripheral." By examining the interplay of media and rurality, Barney's work sheds light on the biases that shape our understanding of urban and rural geographies, showing how technological flows are as crucial to rural areas as they are to urban centers.

While many dark-sky advocates rely on the sublime wonders of the starry night to imagine pristine darkness as a spiritual resource free from the entanglement of contemporary technologies, in reality, the contemporary star gazer, like the modern farmer, is embedded in a vast array of media networks and digital technologies. Indeed, it could be argued that modern media technologies have profoundly enhanced the experience of sky gazing, transforming it from a passive way of viewing into an interactive and enriching pursuit dependent on various information flows. Smartphone apps like *Stellarium* and *Star Walk* act as portable planetariums, utilizing GPS and augmented reality to identify celestial objects and provide detailed information about their characteristics and mythology. Online resources such as interactive sky maps and virtual observatories grant access to high-quality telescopes and images from around the world, enabling users to explore the cosmos from their homes. Furthermore, advancements in digital cameras and image processing techniques empower amateur astrophotographers to capture stunning images of the night sky, revealing details invisible to the naked eye. Finally, social media and online forums connect astronomy enthusiasts worldwide, fostering knowledge sharing and collaborative learning. By bridging geographical boundaries and enhancing observational capabilities, these technologies do not sever rural people from media technologies; instead, they have democratized access to the wonders of the universe, making skygazing a more accessible and *highly mediated* pursuit for people of all ages and backgrounds.

Networks: Interwoven Rural and Urban Realities

The idea of the pristine night as an isolated geography neglects the intricate networks that connect many places, from the rural heartland to the urban center. The glow of distant city lights bleed into the rural periphery, urban anxieties about crime and safety shape perceptions about the night, even in quiet communities, and increasingly the flows of digital data blur the temporal boundaries traditionally associated with rural and urban life. As the geographer Doreen Massey argues, under globalization rural, suburban, and urban areas are not separate entities but integral parts of a single, dynamic spatial system characterized by mutual flows of people, goods, capital, and ideas. Crucial to this understanding of the relationality of geography is Massey's (1991) idea of 'a global sense of place.' She writes:

> One way of thinking about place is as particular moments in [...] intersecting social relations, nets of which have over time been constructed, laid down, interacted with one another, decayed and renewed. Some of these relations will be, as it were, contained within the place; others will stretch beyond it, tying any particular locality into wider relations and processes in which other places are implicated too. [...] The global is in the local in the very process of the formation of the local (1994, 120).

Massey's adage that "the local is the global" is vividly illustrated by the satellite internet industry's efforts to connect remote regions, a seemingly positive development that carries many hidden costs. Bridging the digital divide, satellite internet empowers individuals in isolated and rural locations to participate in the global economy, access information, and connect with people worldwide. This localized access fosters cultural exchange, knowledge sharing, and economic opportunities that transcend geographical boundaries. Furthermore, the development and deployment of satellite technology requires international collaboration, involving urban companies and researchers from across the globe. The very infrastructure that enables local connectivity is a testament to the interconnection between urban and rural places. However, this interconnectedness comes at a price. The proliferation of satellites contributes to light pollution, disrupting astronomical observation and impacting the natural behaviour of nocturnal wildlife. The increasing density of objects in orbit also raises the risk of collisions, generating space debris that further exacerbates light pollution and poses a threat to other satellites. Thus, the satellite internet industry exemplifies the complex interplay between "country and city," where advancements aimed at benefiting remote communities also contribute to the growing global problem of light pollution.

By addressing these contradictions, this book looks to dispel the myth of pristine darkness—the nostalgic idea that in order to save the starry night we need to return to a pre-industrial night sky imagined as completely untouched and free from all traces of human civilizations. This romanticized notion not only ignores how humans have always interacted with and altered the night, from the first campfires to the gas lights that illuminated modern Paris, but it fails to recognize the ongoing transformations taking place to the night sky. While light pollution from industrialization and urbanization has undoubtedly intensified, the idea of a pure, unaltered night sky is a fallacy that obscures the complex and continuous relationship between humans and the nocturnal environment.

Chapter Summaries

Chapter One: Nature documentaries have long captivated audiences by blending education with the visual spectacle of the natural world. Over time, they have evolved into a sophisticated genre that combines technological innovation and storytelling to reveal nature's "exotic" and "pristine" wonders. Despite their focus on diurnal activities, advancements in low-light, infrared, and heat-sensing technologies have enabled the rise of what I call the "nocturnal nature documentary," a sub-genre of environmental media that explores how ecosystems thrive in darkness. Analyzing recent series like *Night on Earth* and *Earth at Night in Color*, I show how these docuseries use new night technologies to illuminate the mysterious behaviors of nocturnal wildlife, offering audiences an enriched understanding of the natural world after dark. This chapter will also introduce the concept of the "astronomical uncanny" to explain how nocturnal documentaries challenge traditional portrayals of nature. Through an exploration of three modes of astronomical uncanny, I will argue that by emphasizing the interconnectedness of urban and rural ecosystems and the technological mediation of nature, nocturnal nature documentaries not only avoid depicting darkness as something separate from urban technological society, but through its foregrounding of modern media fosters a deeper appreciation of the complexity and vulnerability of life after dark.

Chapter Two: This chapter explores the rise of astro-tourism, a form of ecotourism designed to preserve "pristine" dark skies and counteract the light pollution caused by urbanization. While dark sky advocates promote the beauty and cultural significance of the night sky to inspire conservation, the chapter critiques the limitations of relying on aesthetic appeals alone to address systemic environmental and technological challenges. Specifically, I will analyze Tyler Nordgren's promotional materials for stargazing in American Dark Sky Parks. Drawing on nineteenth-century Romantic ideals and frontier nostalgia, Nordgren's posters depict the night sky as an ancient, serene refuge disconnected from modern urban life. Situating Nordgren's work within the historical myth of "pristine wilderness," I show how this esthetic approach perpetuates a binary between nature and human intervention that ignores the historical and ongoing transformations of the night sky. While his imagery evokes wonder, it risks fostering escapism rather than meaningful engagement with the systemic causes of light pollution. Furthermore, by framing the starry night as timeless and unchanging, the campaign ignores the effects of technological expansion, such as the proliferation of satellite trails, which are increasingly visible even in the darkest skies. The chapter concludes by calling for a new approach to astro-tourism that combines an appreciation for the night's beauty with a critical awareness of its transformation by human activity. Drawing inspiration from practices like space archaeology and citizen science, it advocates for visual strategies highlighting the material and technological realities shaping the night sky, offering a more grounded and inclusive conservation vision.

Chapter Three: This chapter builds upon some of the ideas in Chapter Two, especially how satellites and their proliferation have transformed the night sky. While some view satellites as visual pollutants disrupting the pristine beauty of the cosmos, others, like artist Trevor Paglen, use artworks to critique the invisibility of these technologies. In the first part of the chapter, I explore how some astrophotographers consider satellite trails as contaminants that detract from the sublime, ancestral experience of the night sky. Using advanced AI tools, they digitally erase these trails to restore an idealized image of "pristine" darkness. While these methods preserve the "pristine" aesthetics of astrophotography, I critique this practice for reinforcing neoliberal governance frameworks. By "cleaning up" visual evidence of satellite pollution, these methods obscure the broader sociopolitical and ecological consequences of space exploitation, perpetuating a romanticized and depoliticized vision of the cosmos. In contrast, Paglen's projects, such as *The Last Pictures* and *Orbital Reflector*, foreground the physical and political realities of satellites, showing how powerful institutional forces control outer space. The chapter ends by arguing that art offers critical counter-visual strategies to expose the material and political dimensions of space infrastructure. By emphasizing the entanglements of satellites with capitalism, governance, and ecology, these artistic interventions challenge the myths of purity and progress, advocating for a more inclusive approach to humanity's relationship with the night sky.

Chapter Four: While initiatives to preserve natural darkness in designated "dark-sky" areas are valuable, they may not be enough to sway urban populations towards sustainable lighting practices. This chapter argues that interactive digital art, particularly the work of the collective teamLab, offers a powerful alternative by cultivating an appreciation for "artificial darkness" within urban environments. Historically, darkness has often been associated with negativity, but scholars are increasingly recognizing its potential for fostering wonder and social intimacy. While this re-evaluation often focuses on natural darkness, the concept of "artificial darkness"—darkness created through technological means—has not been given much attention.

Analyzing the installations of teamLab, I will show how the interplay of artificial light and darkness can create immersive installations that celebrate darkness. Their works, such as those found in their Borderless Museum, transform urban spaces into sensory-rich environments where the interplay of light and shadow evokes a sense of awe reminiscent of stargazing. These installations, often interactive and participatory, not only offer a fresh perspective on the aesthetic qualities of darkness but also foster social connection by encouraging shared experiences and co-creation. By using darkness as a medium, teamLab collapses the traditional distance between viewer and artwork, prioritizing emotional connection over static authenticity. This aligns with a growing body of scholarship emphasizing the importance of multisensory engagement in fostering meaningful connections with art. Ultimately, teamLab's installations offer a compelling model for appreciating darkness in an increasingly urbanized world. By creating accessible, inclusive, and emotionally resonant experiences with artificial darkness, they demonstrate that the wonder of the night sky can be reimagined within the city.

Chapter Five: This chapter explores the Arctic night as a contested space shaped by ongoing colonial processes, including extraction capitalism, technological expansion, and cultural erasure. Through the idea of astro-colonization, I critique the way colonial media frame the Arctic night as an isolated refuge, showing how this idea of pristine darkness is intricately connected to contemporary forms of racism and resource exploitation. Analyzing three forms Indigenous media, I hope to challenge some of the prevailing colonial myths about the Arctic night: first, Jennie Williams' *Nalujuk Night* will be used to counter the perception of the polar night as isolating; instead the night is shown in the film to foster communal bonds through nocturnal rituals; second, Tanya Tagaq's *Split Tooth* depicts the Arctic night as both a colonial space of harm and a site for healing, where the narrator reclaims her body and ancestral ties through an erotic encounter with the Northern Lights; and finally, HBO's *True Detective: Night Country* critiques systemic violence against Indigenous women, subverting the trope of Indigenous victimhood by portraying Indigenous women as active agents of justice against extractive industries. Through these media examples, I argue that decolonizing the Arctic night requires resisting these colonial myths while centering Indigenous traditions that view darkness as a vital, interconnected space for resilience, storytelling, and cultural survival.

Chapter One

THE NOCTURNAL NATURE DOCUMENTARY

Introduction

Since the emergence of cinema in the late nineteenth century, nature documentaries have become one of the most prolific and engaging genres for sharing scientific knowledge about the natural world (Aufderheide, 2007). Over their long and sometimes contentious history, nature films have not only offered audiences mesmerizing views of the Earth's most remote and "exotic" landscapes, but they continue to uncover nature's hidden wonders, blending spectacle with education to highlight the richness of nonhuman life. Much like the iconic Pale Blue Dot image taken by Voyager One, which depicts the Earth as a wondrous speck set against the vastness of the cosmos, nature documentaries do more than describe the mechanics of nature; they reveal worlds beyond our everyday experience, sparking awe and curiosity about the planet we call home. As Carl Sagan (2011) writes about the famous Blue Dot, "Look again at that dot. That's here. That's home. That's us [...] The Earth is a very small stage in a vast cosmic arena."

Even though nature documentaries have used a wide range of storytelling techniques to foster an appreciation of nature—from the sublime portrayal of underwater worlds in *Blue Planet II* to the humorous exploration of the human body in *Life on Us*—they have had much less to say about the natural world after dark. While technical limitations are not the sole reason for this oversight, the challenges of capturing low-light imagery with earlier camera technology have contributed to the genre's focus on daytime scenes. As a result, the mysterious and vibrant world of nocturnal ecosystems, which truly come to life under the cover of darkness, has been an under-explored theme in nature documentaries.

However, with recent advancements in low-light, infrared, and heat-sensing technologies, which allow filmmakers to capture nighttime scenes with remarkable clarity, often using nothing but moonlight, the nature documentary is experiencing a nocturnal boom. Featured in several high-profile, blue-chip nature series, including *The Dark: Nature's Nighttime World*, *Night of the Lion*, *Night on Earth*, and *Earth At Night in Color*, these cutting-edge technologies have paved the way for what I call the "nocturnal nature documentary," a new subgenre that brings the hidden nocturnal world into the spotlight. Like other blue-chip nature films, which depict nature as a wondrous paradise of breathtaking beauty, nocturnal nature documentaries reveal the unique and awe-inspiring behaviors of nocturnal plants and animals, offering viewers a richer, more comprehensive understanding of the natural world after dark.

Yet, while the nocturnal nature documentary shares much in common with many mainstream nature series, its focus on the technological mediation of darkness brings about significant changes to the genre, especially the aesthetic conventions associated with high-profile, blue-chip nature films. Throughout history and across cultures, nighttime has been linked to the supernatural, the unknown, and the mystical. Myths, folklore, and legends often depict the night as a time when supernatural beings—ghosts, spirits, and monsters—roam, reinforcing the idea that darkness is a mysterious and potentially dangerous force. While the nocturnal nature documentary still abides by many of the conventions of realism and is dedicated to promoting scientific knowledge, many of the episodes discussed in this chapter tap into the night's supernatural associations, infusing scientific naturalism with a sense of the weird and the strange.

To draw out the significance of these changes to the nature documentary, in this chapter, I draw on insights from the ecological uncanny, a robust set of environmental theories that emphasis the strangeness of nature, to explore how the nocturnal nature documentary's portrayal of the night as a place teeming with strange and fascinating creatures not only highlights the importance of preserving dark skies but also challenges many of the dominant representations of nature in traditional blue-chip films. While series like *Earth at Night in Color* and *Night on Earth* borrow significantly from the blue-chip tradition—particularly in terms of high production values and the use of celebrity ambassadors, their approach to depicting darkness introduces transformative aesthetic and narrative conventions that set the subgenre apart. I refer to this representational approach as the "astronomical uncanny," an aesthetic approach to nighttime that highlights the strange and perplexing connections between terrestrial ecologies and starry skies. As I will show, by drawing on the night's associations with the bizarre, nocturnal nature documentaries offer an alternative way to convey the importance of preserving darkness. This approach not only deepens our understanding of how nonhumans experience darkness but also underscores the need to harness new technologies to understand the extensive harm urban light pollution inflicts on rural nocturnal environments.

From Home to the Unhomely: The Evolution of the Nature Film

Throughout its history, nature documentaries have consistently embraced new technologies—ranging from the introduction of color television in the 1950s to the advent of portable sound recorders in the 1960s—to shape their genre conventions and aesthetic styles (Collins, 2017; Horak, 2006). Among these, the blue-chip nature documentary has remained the most popular and commercially successful format (Louson, 2021; Scott, 2003). Frequently associated with the iconic British naturalist Sir David Attenborough, blue-chip documentaries are characterized by their paradoxical mix of high-tech, sophisticated entertainment with portrayals of nature as an untouched, pristine wilderness. While the blue-chip genre has evolved over time, its key features include: the use of authoritative, almost god-like voice-over narration; a commitment to scientific realism as the core principle of nature communication; the deployment of cutting-edge visual and audio technologies, such as IMAX's high-definition cameras and projectors; a heavy focus on close-up shots of charismatic megafauna; the application of familial metaphors to depict animal societies; and a portrayal of nature as an unspoiled paradise, often achieved by masking the production process and omitting any trace of human influence.

In his book *Reel Nature: America's Romance with Wildlife*, environmental historian Gregg Mitman traces the blue-chip film's depiction of nature as pristine wilderness back to the early 1900s and the rise of the Nature Park movement in the United States. According to Mitman, to protect nature, rural "wilderness" had to be imagined as a pure, unspoiled spiritual resource, free from the contaminating influences of industrialized civilization. In this framework, while urban cultures provided material and technological progress, unchecked urban development was seen as a threat to the preservation of "pure" nature, potentially leading to its degradation and impoverishment. As Mitman writes:

> Nature films, naturalistic habitat displays, and animal theme parks like Disney's Animal Kingdom capitalize on our desire to be close to nature, yet curiously removed from it. By making animals into spectacle, rather than beings we engage with in work and play, nature films and other recreations of nature reinforce this dichotomy of humans and nature. In nature as spectacle, the animal kingdom exists solely to be observed, objectified, and enjoyed. We have our world and they have theirs. This voyeurism precludes any meaningful exchange because we remain at a physically and emotionally safe distance, far removed from the shared

> labor of animals and humans, whose interactions have made such vicarious experiences possible. We no longer work with animals, we predominantly watch them. (206)

To construct this idea of nature as an observable spectacle separated from human life, many blue-chip films erase all technological signs of the contemporary age by making nature resemble the deep and ancient past. "Reel" nature is, in short, refers to nature as it existed before the emergence of human civilization. According to Mitman, this aesthetic feat requires significant behind-the-scenes labor to erase all signs of modern life. Disney, a pioneering force in early nature documentaries, played a crucial role in fostering this nostalgic longing for a primeval natural world. For instance, in its True-Life Adventures series, Disney frequently used intimate, close-up shots of charismatic animals to portray the moral value of untainted wilderness and the dangers of an encroaching urban life set to destroy the beauty of nature. However, to maintain this image of vulnerable and endearing animals, the technical tools of production—especially the telephoto lenses that created the illusion of closeness—had to be hidden, along with any visible traces of humans.

In addition to the challenge of concealing film's technological apparatus, nature series like Disney's grappled with another paradox: how to tell relatable stories that simultaneously celebrated nature's "exoticness" while masking its cruelty and indifference. As media scholar Cynthia Chris (2006) points out, nature documentaries often resolve this paradox by domesticating animal sexuality. According to Chris, a scientifically accurate portrayal of animal sexuality, which might include polygamy or violent competition, was deemed unsuitable for Disney's audiences. Instead, the animal world was recast to fit the social conventions of the nuclear family, with clear demarcations between male and female roles.

While blue-chip films like those from Disney tame "wild" nature through well-known tropes—especially the charismatic animal family—recently, there has been a shift toward ecological discourses that approach "nature" from the perspectives of the weird, the uncanny, and the strange (Bigelow, 2023; Fernando, 2022). Prominent ecological thinker Timothy Morton (2013, 2021), a key figure in object-oriented philosophy, articulates this transition by emphasizing how ecological awareness cannot be reduced to the familiarity of human experience. Morton critiques phenomenological approaches that root ecological thought in the human sensorium and its local attachments to nature. For him, this "homely" view of nature fails to apprehend the wonderfully weird and unpredictable nature of ecology. Rather than portraying nature as a good-natured, holistic entity as Disney does, Morton describes nature as queer—"catastrophic, monstrous, nonholistic, and dislocated, not organic, coherent, or authoritative" (2010, p. 275). Nature, in Morton's view, is made up of "strange strangers"—entities imbued with irreducible differences that resist simple categorization.

Similarly, in his influential book *Hyperobjects*, Morton discusses the uncanny nature of vast ecological entities like climate change, nuclear waste, and light pollution, which cannot be comprehended directly by human experience and, as such, remain eerily dissonant. These hyperobjects, which are massively distributed across time and space, destabilize the familiar ways humans perceive and interact with the world. Although we can engage with hyperobjects at a local level or scale, they consistently exceed our sensory capacity, producing a gap between our human-centric experience of the world and the vast, complex systems that impact everyday life. This unbridgeable gap contributes to an unsettling uncanniness at the core of our human-centric reality, as we must accept that our actions are bound up with forces that extend far beyond our immediate experiences.

While Morton's ideas on ecological strangeness have gained prominence, other ecological thinkers have also employed concepts like the weird, the uncanny, and the strange to grapple with the distressing impacts some human cultures have on the environment (Diogo et al., 2017; Pay, 2019; Giblett, 2019). In the remaining sections of this chapter, I examine how nocturnal nature documentaries employ new night vision technologies to create a range of uncanny aesthetic and narrative conventions that transform how the blue-chip documentary mediates nature. Specifically, I outline three different modes of the uncanny that are featured predominantly in the nocturnal nature series. For example, rather than hiding the camera's intrusive presence, the nocturnal nature documentary reminds viewers of the camera's eerie ability to see in the dark; instead of celebrating the nuclear family, with its relatable social roles, it delves into the strange and "alien" behaviors of nocturnal creatures; and instead of upholding a binary system that separates nature and culture, the nocturnal nature documentary reveals the unsettling entanglements between rural ecosystems and urban environments.

Uncanny One: Seeing in the Dark

In his work on photography, German cultural critic Walter Benjamin highlighted how cameras can uncover aspects of reality that are hidden from human perception (Smith and Sliwinski, 2017). For Benjamin (1999; 2008), the camera possesses an "optical unconscious" that surpasses human sight by slowing down time or revealing hidden details through magnification. As he (1999) writes:

> For it is another nature which speaks to the camera rather than to the eye: "other" above all in the sense that a space informed by human

> consciousness gives way to a space informed by the unconscious. Whereas it is a commonplace that, for example, we have some idea what is involved in the act of walking (if only in general terms), we have no idea at all what happens during the fraction of a second when a person actually takes a step. Photography, with its devices of slow motion and enlargement, reveals the secret. It is through photography that we first discover the existence of this optical unconscious, just as we discover the instinctual unconscious through psychoanalysis. (510–12)

Similarly, early film theorist Rudolf Arnheim noted that the camera's ability to capture nature's intricate details, such as those of tiny insects, humbles the human mind by showing the complexity of nature that resides beyond our ordinary vision. Arnheim's philosophy of film, which suggests that the camera provides access to a world designed independently of human observation, challenges our assumptions about the role optical technologies play in advancing human knowledge. "Nothing is more humbling," wrote Arnheim, "than to look with a strong magnifying glass at an insect so tiny that the naked eye sees only the barest speck and to discover nevertheless it is sculpted and articulated and striped with the same care and imagination as a zebra. Apparently, it does not occur to nature whether or not a creature is within our range of vision, and the suspicion arises that even the zebra was not designed for our benefit" (160).

Benjamin and Arnheim's insights into the augmentative capabilities of camera technologies are a useful starting point for discussing the eerie way nocturnal nature documentaries "see in the dark." Human night vision is notably poor, but, as Benjamin and Arnheim remind us, technological advancements can uncover realities that remain hidden from human sight. In the nocturnal nature documentaries discussed in this chapter, this enhancement of human vision is framed as an uncanny experience, wherein night vision not only uncovers strange worlds but recalibrates the human senses, creating new and foreign phenomenological experiences.

For example, in the first episode of *Night on Earth*, low-light cameras are used to track a group of cheetahs as darkness settles over the African plains (Figure 1). A voice-over narrator explains that what viewers are about to see has never been captured on film. Traditionally, cheetahs were believed to have poor night vision, restricting their hunting activities to daylight hours. However, this group of cheetahs challenges that belief, demonstrating they can hunt under moonlit conditions. While the revelation of cheetahs' nocturnal hunting capabilities is fascinating, the way in which the viewer learns about these new animal behaviors is equally remarkable. As night descends and the sun sets, the camera unveils a perplexing and wonderous sight: the African

Figure 1. Low-light camera showing cheetah's hunting under moonlight. (Screen capture of Netflix's *Night on Earth.*)

plains, bathed in total darkness, are rendered to appear as though it were daytime. Like other blue-chip films, the voice-over narrator in this scene speaks with scientific authority. However, the narrator's emphasis on the camera's ability to transform night into day overlooks the true peculiarity of the scene. What is uncanny and strange about being able to see cheetah's hunting in the dark is not merely the way the camera is able to create clear and vivid images with very little available light, but how the sequence creates a surreal montage of "illuminated darkness." As Mark Fisher (2016) notes, "the weird is that which does not belong. The weird brings to the familiar something which ordinarily lies beyond it and cannot be reconciled with the homely. The form that is most appropriate to the weird is montage—the joining of two or more things which do not belong together." Undoubtedly, low-light cameras allow viewers to see the cheetahs hunt in the dark with remarkable clarity; the African plains appear as if it were daytime. But what the narrator misses is that alongside this feat of illumination is the construction of a weird, simulated landscape that still bears traces of night: the moon above shines bright, the stars twinkle in the sky, and shadowy darkness looms in the periphery. The result is an uncanny overlap of incongruous images, as the viewer confronts a strange virtual landscape that cojoins night and day.

Similarly, in the episode "Jungle Nights," heat-sensing cameras are not only presented as scientific tools revealing new knowledge about nocturnal animal behaviors but also as "phantom technologies" that present the animal world at night as hauntingly beautiful. The episode, which follows a group of scientists who use advanced thermal imaging technology to monitor orangutans as they navigate their forest habitat in the dark, provides an incredible glimpse

Figure 2. Thermal image of an orangutan. (Screen capture of Netflix's *Night on Earth.*)

into the nocturnal behavior of these remarkable creatures (Figure 2). Since thermal imaging converts the temperature of objects into electronic images, the thermal cameras transform the orangutans into ghostly figures, their warm glowing bodies set against the cooler backdrop of their surroundings. Highlighting how these intelligent primates use their environment at night, whether it's searching for food, moving among the treetops, or settling down to rest in nests they construct high in the canopy, the episode demonstrates the unprecedented way new cameras can unveil hidden facets of nature, as the glowing images allow scientists to see the animal's movements and behaviors in unprecedented detail.

While the episode underscores the importance of using technology to seek out new knowledge about the animal world, the use of heat-sensing cameras adds a dramatic and immersive layer to the storytelling, offering a perspective that wouldn't be possible with traditional filming methods. By presenting the orangutans in an ethereal way, as both beautiful creatures with untapped capabilities and ghostly apparitions on the verge of extinction, the show uses the uncanniness of the night to underscore the importance of preserving their natural habitats in the face of deforestation and other threats. In this way, aesthetics and epistemology combine to show the viewer the value of darkness.

In addition to creating striking representations of animals and their habitats, the nocturnal nature documentary portrays "seeing in the dark" as a sensory-rich experience that heightens the body's vulnerabilities. Tim Edensor (2015a, 2015b), in his ethnographic exploration of nighttime geographies, characterizes night as a realm of eerie dissonance, where sensations of gloom and darkness recalibrate human perceptions. As night descends, vision—the primary sense during the day—diminishes, necessitating the enhancement of other senses, like touch and hearing to compensate for the reduced visual clarity. Similarly, Gregory Bateson (1972) notes that a clear sense of self arises from the perception of one's separation from others, a distinction made possible by the brightness and clarity of light. However, in darkness, this clear sense of self weakens, blurring the lines between the self and the external environment. This results in a more permeable nighttime self, increasingly sensitive to otherness. In these phenomenological interpretations of darkness, nighttime serves, as Will Straw (2015) suggests, as a substance that causes things to vanish.

In the nocturnal nature documentary, this split between the vulnerabilities of darkness and the stability of light is not so clear-cut. While night vision technologies enable the filmmaker to "see in the dark," and therefore belong to a long succession of artificial forms of illumination that reduce the risks associated with darkness, working in the dark nonetheless exposes filmmakers to an assortment of unknown dangers. Throughout *Night on Earth,* for example, the viewer is consistently reminded of the inherent hazards of filming in darkness, where the night obscures the clarity of shapes, objects, and colors, effectively exposing filmmakers to new dangers. In the first episode, the peril of being engulfed in darkness is candidly addressed by a camera crew as they track an elusive family of cheetahs. Since even the slightest amount of light would scare the animals away, the crew is compelled to navigate the challenging terrain in complete darkness. Relying solely on a pair of night vision goggles for guidance, the driver describes the pursuit as a menacing game of chicken, forced to rely on unpredictable guesswork to prevent crashing the vehicle. In another episode, a bat researcher is seen moving through a series of dangerous caverns, depending only on a thermal camera to illuminate his path. Much like the cheetah episode, the researcher is shown confronting the precariousness of the dark, using just a sliver of illumination to navigate the caves safely.

In these and other scenes, night vision is portrayed as a double-edged sword. On one hand, by extending the capabilities of human vision, night vision technology empowers filmmakers to explore uncharted landscapes and ecosystems. Areas such as dark caves, abandoned settlements, the depths of the sea, and dense forests—once considered inaccessible threats at night—become open to exploration. Equipped with thermal or infrared cameras, filmmakers acquire a peculiar set of eyes that make these elusive and daunting environments attainable. Yet, these accentuations of artificial illumination do not destroy the exhilarating vulnerabilities of darkness. Rather, as Edensor (2015a, 2015b) writes, navigating gloom "contains potential for enchantment, a condition that fuels the potential to enhance playfulness, exhilarates through encounter with the unexpected in the realm of the mundane." In the nocturnal nature documentary, the prospect of "seeing in the dark" becomes the precondition for encountering something different, even slightly dangerous, in the dark, a call to explore the unknown wonders of the night.

Uncanny Two: Seeing the World Like a Mantis Shrimp

Anthropologist Tim Ingold (2021) suggests that observing nature provides an education in attention. The environment, characterized by its constant unfolding and dynamic changes, continually offers signals and clues about the nature of reality. From the gentle movement of clouds above to the faint rustle of twigs in a forest, nature presents a complex and subtle communication system awaiting discovery. These signs, often hidden from the untrained eye, are not merely symbols to be deciphered; they are effective and sentient indicators that can teach the patient observer much about what it means to exist in the world.

Throughout the nocturnal nature documentary, night vision technology allows viewers to enhance their experiences with darkness, gaining insight into how scientists utilize this technology to deepen their understanding of the "alien" ways nonhumans sense and interact with their environments. For instance, in episode four of *Night on Earth,* a crew of filmmakers venture into the shadowy depths of the deep sea to explore the eerie polarized vision of the Tiger Mantis Shrimp (Figure 3). This creature, described as the ultimate ambush predator, is imagined as a prehistoric monster that possesses the most sophisticated optical system in the animal kingdom. Each of its eyes can independently detect high dynamic range, and in total darkness, it perceives polarized light waves—a superpower sixth sense that allows it to locate prey with pinpoint accuracy. Similarly, in episode three, the narrator introduces

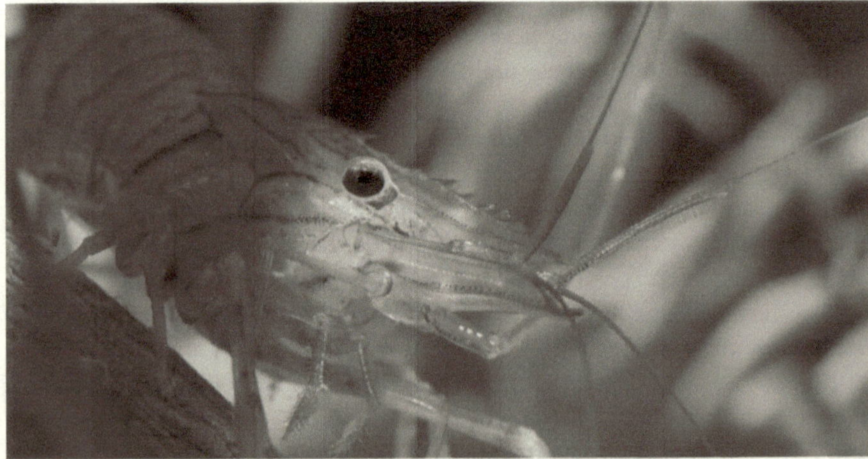

Figure 3. Image of a tiger mantis shrimp. (Screen capture of Netflix's *Night on Earth.*)

Figure 4. Image of bioluminescent fungi. (Screen capture of Netflix's *Night on Earth.*)

the viewer to the fascinating world of bioluminescent fungi (Figure 4). These self-illuminating mushrooms emit an enchanting green and blue glow to attract invertebrates, which aid in spreading their reproductive spores. The episode also explores the carnivorous habits of pitcher plants. For years, the method by which these plants captured their prey remained a mystery. However, using cameras capable of detecting ultraviolet light, it is revealed that pitcher plants use light waves to ensnare insects at night, acting as dazzling "beacons of eerie light" to lure them in.

Through these scenes, the nocturnal documentary crafts a bewildering version of nature that evokes feelings of wonderment. Unlike the domestic metaphors employed in earlier blue-chip films, these "alien" nocturnal experiences remind viewers of the varied ways darkness is perceived beyond human vision, revealing aspects of the night that elude human understanding. This representation of the night resonates with the work of Swedish zoologist Johan Eklöf (2023), whose research on light pollution highlights the unique ways animals perceive and interact with darkness. Speaking about the otherworldly nature of the ocean, Eklöf writes, "The dark and unknown deep ocean is a world completely different from our own, where light only comes for short visits. Life shows itself in flashing streaks and blinking nodes, and in between this, it is completely black. To our eyes it would be perceived as a ghostly and foreign dimension, a place not meant for us."

By presenting nature at night as an uncanny realm teeming with strangeness, the nocturnal nature documentary aligns more closely with the weirdness of speculative realism than the scientific naturalism of many blue-chip films. "One of the key features of the Speculative Turn," Levi Bryant (2010) suggests, "is precisely that the move toward realism is not a move toward the limitations of common sense but quite often a turn toward the downright bizarre." As a broad philosophical movement that asserts that the world does not revolve around human perception, speculative realism supports the idea that non-human entities possess their own forms of agency, complexity, and "weirdness" that are not contingent on human understanding. However, while I appreciate the speculative turn's desire to understand nature as a unique and unknowable wonder, this may not be the best perspective for assessing the role scientific instruments, like thermal cameras, play in understanding and preserving darkness.

For example, Object-Oriented Ontology (OOO), a branch of speculative realism, often critiques science's philosophical assumptions about reality, especially the reductive and anthropocentric tendencies of scientific inquiry and its treatment of objects as secondary to human access or utility (Harman, 2010). Since science frequently frames the natural world in terms of its relevance to human understanding or utility, OOO rejects this anthropocentric bias, emphasizing that objects—whether they are rocks, bacteria, or galaxies—exist in their own right, with their own realities that are not contingent upon human perception or analysis. This dismissal of science and the role instruments play in "knowing" natural objects stems primarily from OOO's central idea, which is that objects "withdraw" from human access—they always retain an aspect of their existence that cannot be fully known or experienced. Science, however, operates on the assumption that objects can be understood given enough data or analysis. OOO critiques this assumption as overly optimistic and dismissive of the deeper, hidden dimensions of reality.

Perhaps the most relevant OOO scholar for assessing the ways nonhumans perceive darkness is Ian Bogost. In his work on alien phenomenology, Bogost (2012) revisits Thomas Nagel's famous speculative essay, "What it's like to be a Bat," to criticize the natural sciences for their poor understanding of how other life forms experience the world. As Bogost argues, "Counterintuitive though it may seem, the characterization of an experience through supposedly external mechanisms leads us farther from, not closer to, an understanding of the experience of an entity." Rather than focusing on how scientific tools, like infrared cameras, help scientists grasp other lifeforms' perceptions, Bogost draws on Harman's object-oriented philosophy to claim that the sense-making abilities of creatures like mantis shrimp or fungi exist in a self-contained and inaccessible realm. Even Eklof, whose work resides firmly within the natural sciences, bemoans how the limitation of human vision prevents us from directly experiencing the strange nocturnal perceptions of nonhumans. Echoing the language of many speculative realists, he writes:

It is fascinating to imagine how nocturnal animals experience their existence in the dark, how their brains interpret sensory stimuli. In my vicinity, hundreds of normally invisible white flowers called Nottingham catchfly glitter when the moon shows itself. It is subtly beautiful, but for animals with sensitivity to the ultraviolet spectrum, the ground shines like a fluorescent dance floor. As humans— with our senses' limitations— though we know about these animals' visual faculties, we can never understand the real experience. Filters in cameras or visual enhancement through other machines let us have an inkling, but we can never completely see with the eyes of insects or cats.

Although we can never fully grasp how mantis shrimp perceive darkness, empirical research and instruments provide us with more than mere "caricatures" of nonhuman perception. Furthermore, while the focus on human limitations in accessing nonhuman perception can challenge our anthropocentric views, philosophical discussions alone fall short of addressing practical issues, such as effectively safeguarding species that rely on dark environments. We may not fully understand how baby turtles interpret moonlight, but technologies and empirical observations offer important frameworks for comprehending the harmful impacts of light pollution on nonhuman life. Hence, asserting that genuine awe and wonderment arises solely from the inaccessibility of nonhumans undermines the genuine marvel that can still emerge from approximating the visual experiences of different animals. For example, even though humans cannot directly observe the ultraviolet spectrum, technologies like cameras can serve as proxies, enabling us to gain insights into nonhuman perceptions.

For my concept of the uncanny night, I rely on the work of Steven Shaviro (2014), who suggests that we should view nonhuman perception not just as an epistemological matter but through a "democracy of sensation," the idea that aesthetic interactions between entities are just as important as epistemological certainties. As Shaviro writes, "If all entities in here in the world 'in the same sense,' we must describe this inherence in the same way for all of them." To counteract the prevalent anthropocentrism, Shaviro argues that we should embrace anthropomorphism. Just as humans are transformed by their affective encounters with other things, scientific tools, such as night cameras, provide distinct aesthetic ways of perceiving the world, which actually enrich our insights into how nonhumans are affected by night. As Shaviro explains, "Finitude, therefore, means not only that there are limits to our knowledge of the moon but also—and much more importantly—that there are limits to our independence from the moon." In other words, every object may well be "withdrawn" epistemologically from all the others, but this need not mean that objects are "barricaded behind firewalls."

In the opening episode of *Night on Earth*, viewers are offered a proxy view of the night vision of cheetahs. As the voice-over narrator clarifies, the footage is not a direct representation of feline vision, but rather the perceptual capabilities of a camera designed for low-light conditions. The footage serves as an embodied metaphor, with the camera providing viewers with something akin to the cheetah's night vision. If we were to rely solely on speculative realism, the vision of cheetahs would fade into the background, hidden behind an inaccessible barrier. However, Shaviro's aesthetic approach reminds us that all things share in the affective and aesthetic translation of the world into images and sensations; and that though media technologies may never provide us with direct access to the nonhuman, they can nonetheless reveal the myriad ways in which the world presents itself, highlighting the wonder and allure inherent in appearances.

Uncanny Three: The Return of the Repressed

The final mode of uncanniness involves the return of the repressed. Like the Freudian uncanny (1919), which describes the unsettling resurgence of repressed thoughts, the nocturnal uncanny acknowledges the sudden and striking reappearance of the "undesirable nonhumans" modern lighting systems strive to suppress. Writing about the harms of climate heating, Amitav Ghosh (2016) encapsulates this sense of uncanniness well when he states: "No other word comes close to expressing the strangeness of what is unfolding around us. For these changes are not merely strange in the sense of being unknown or alien; their uncanniness lies precisely in the fact that in these encounters, we recognize something we had turned away from: that is to say, the presence and proximity of the nonhuman."

For much of Earth's history, life has evolved in sync with the natural transition between day and night. However, with the rise of the so-called 24-hour society, which keeps environments constantly illuminated, we find ourselves in a new evolutionary stage with little understanding of how plants and animals will deal with the widespread increase in artificial light. And what we do know offers little comfort. Eklöf notes, "No less than a third of all vertebrates and almost two-thirds of all invertebrates are nocturnal, and so most of nature's activity—mating, hunting, decomposing, and pollinating—occurs after we humans fall asleep at night." Given that many species rely on darkness for their survival, it is not surprising that, as urban areas continue to expand, humans will increasingly encounter the strange and uncanny phenomena that Ghosh highlights.

In contrast to many blue-chip documentaries that promote the idea that vast stretches of untouched wilderness remain intact, the nocturnal nature documentary directly addresses these unsettling intrusions, highlighting the unusual connections between nocturnal animals and urban life. For instance, in one of the more chilling episodes of *Night on Earth*, the clash between the urban and the rural is starkly illustrated through the often-violent interactions between displaced leopards and the residents of Mumbai. As urban expansion encroaches on the leopards' hunting grounds, these nocturnal hunters are compelled to hunt within the crowded city streets. Drawing inspiration from horror films, the episode presents the leopard as a stealthy urban predator, causing the city dwellers to remain perpetually on high alert. In another episode set in South Africa, sharks are depicted as night hunters that utilize the constant illumination of nearby cities to overpower their prey. Meanwhile, in Thailand, one of the most peculiar encounters features long-tailed macaques navigating city streets, seamlessly adopting the 24/7 urban lifestyle of their human neighbors.

While many of these episodes might seem exaggerated or fantastical, the concept of the "return of the repressed" is grounded in biological realities, which highlight the challenges many plants and animals face due to increased urban light pollution. In 2013, for example, scientists became increasingly concerned about an "Insect Collapse," the idea that insect populations are rapidly declining because of urban light pollution. Since half of all insects are nocturnal and need prolonged periods of darkness to reproduce, urban illumination has intensified the "vacuum cleaner effect," where cities attract insects away from rural areas due to their attraction to artificial lights, contributing significantly to the reduction in insect biomass. Similarly, recent findings indicate that many elephant herds are shifting towards new nocturnal behaviors. Nighttime has traditionally posed threats for elephants due to predators like lions and hyenas. However, the increasing threat of poaching, which primarily occurs during daylight hours, has forced elephants to undertake the risks of nocturnal travel to avoid the more substantial danger posed by humans.

One of the most striking instances of urban light pollution negatively affecting wildlife is the annual "Tribute in Light" art installation in New York City, which honors the 9/11 tragedy. This installation features nearly a hundred intense spotlights that beam half a mile into the sky, forming two blue columns of light. While the installation serves as an important memorial for the victims of the terrorist attacks, it also overlaps with the migration of birds heading south. Between 2010 and 2017, researchers noted that the birds are drawn to the bright beams and often spiral around them in disorientation, entranced by their brightness. Moreover, studies reveal that the dense cluster of brightly lit skyscrapers in urban areas can ensnare birds in a maze of lights, complicating their ability to find a way out of the city. The consequences of urban lighting on bird populations are dire, resulting in the deaths of nearly a billion birds annually due to collisions with illuminated structures (Van Doren et al., 2017).

If, as Sandy Isenstadt (2018) suggests, the advent of artificial illumination marked the beginning of a new surveillance system, where the simple on/off switch fostered the illusion of being able to control all the undesirable things associated with darkness, what these "wild" intrusions into the urban night signify is the uncanny failure of modernity's quest to enhance urban security by eliminating rural darkness. As scientists like Johan Eklof point out, we still have much to learn about the impact of widespread illumination on the health and survival of plants and animals. However, as our planet becomes increasingly urbanized and artificial lights grow brighter, one thing is certain: the clear boundary between the wild and the urban will continue to blur. Animals whose habitats are disrupted by urbanization will increasingly adapt to city environments, further challenging our perceptions of where the wild truly resides.

Conclusion

In his review of *Night on Earth*, Steve Greene (2020) argues that the series "taps into one of the fundamental drives that have sustained this prolonged nature doc boom in the first place. It scratches the human need to be reminded that there is more left to discover, that there are still some quasi-mystical elements of nature that science has barely had a chance to observe, much less explain. *Night on Earth* also sprinkles in some lingering views of plant life and other observable astronomical occurrences to show that an understanding of this ecosystem involves more than gawking at the fast and the large and the strong. Just like there's no light without the dark, 'Night on Earth' tries to live in the unexpected." Undoubtedly, many recent nature documentaries provide a remarkable exploration of the nocturnal world, transforming the conventional nature documentary format through innovative technology and focusing on the raw beauty of nighttime life. By delving into the intricate connections between urban surroundings and wildlife, it not only broadens our understanding of ecological interrelationships but also emphasizes the need for conservation in an era of rapid urbanization. Ultimately, the series serves as a poignant reminder of the wonders of the natural world and our responsibility to protect it, fostering a deeper appreciation for the complexities of life after dark.

In this chapter, I suggest that the best way to assess these new innovative developments in the nature documentary is through the uncanny. More specifically, I outline three modes of the astronomical uncanny that not only raise awareness about the need to preserve rural darkness but transform some of the conventional ways the blue-chip documentary visualizes nature. Firstly, by utilizing advanced filming techniques and night vision technology to capture scenes that would otherwise be invisible to the human eye, the nocturnal nature documentary not only enriches our visual experience but also transforms our perception of what is considered "natural." The use of thermal imaging and low-light cameras pushes the boundaries of how nature documentaries can present wildlife, giving viewers a glimpse into a realm that challenges human understanding. Secondly, one of the standout features of series like *Night on Earth* and *Earth at Night in Colour* is their focus on nocturnal plants and animals, which are often overlooked in traditional nature documentaries. By illuminating the nocturnal behaviors of creatures such as leopards, bats, and bioluminescent fungi, the series expands our understanding of the ecological interactions that occur after dark. Finally, instead of shying away from exposing the new rural-urban conflicts that emerge from the growing problems of urban light pollution, nocturnal nature documentaries embrace the concept of the return of the repressed, particularly through their portrayal of wildlife navigating urban landscapes. By documenting the interactions of animals like leopards and elephants with urban settings, the series highlights the disruptions caused by human encroachment and the complexities of coexistence in increasingly urbanized environments.

Chapter Two

BEAUTY WON'T SAVE THE STARRY NIGHT: ASTRO-TOURISM AND THE ASTRONOMICAL SUBLIME

Tourism and the Starry Night

While pilgrimages to significant astronomical sites date back to early human civilizations (Brown, 2000), in recent years, astro-tourism has gained popularity as a form of ecotourism aimed at preserving and safeguarding "pristine" dark skies (Escario-Sierra et al., 2022; Farajirad and Beiki, 2015; Fayos-Solà et al., 2014). As urban light pollution rapidly expands, dark skies free from artificial lighting are increasingly rare. It is estimated that nearly 80% of the world's population has never seen the Milky Way (Donahue, 2016), a deprivation of darkness that Paul Virilio (2000) describes as the loss of an ancient cultural heritage. While artificial lighting has undoubtedly brought various benefits to modern societies, the pervasive brightness in most cities today has led many to question the colonization of night by daytime activities (Bogard, 2014; Melbin, 1987).

Like other forms of ecotourism, astro-tourism aims to support rural communities and encourage sustainable connections with nature by presenting itself as a guardian of the night. Encompassing a range of astronomical activities, from stargazing in dark sky parks and preserves to witnessing rare celestial phenomena, such as meteor showers and auroras, astro-tourism seeks to combat the spread of harmful light pollution by highlighting the beauty, cultural significance, and scientific value of the night sky. To carry out this feat, many dark sky destinations draw inspiration for their conservation efforts from the National Park movements of the early twentieth century. For instance, some of the best places to view the Milky Way are located within protected dark areas in the existing nature parks that have recently been certified by the International Dark-Sky Association, a globally recognized organization dedicated to night sky preservation.

In this chapter, I examine the rhetorical mythologies (Barthes, 1999) employed by tourist media to shape the meaning and experiences associated with astronomical destinations. While the growth of astro-tourism has led to a modest body of research, much of it centers on ontological questions about the definition of astro-tourism and its potential for rural development (Blundell et al., 2020; Mitchell and Gallaway, 2019; Silver and Hickey, 2020; Weaver, 2011). However, these studies often overlook crucial questions regarding how image-based promotional media represent the starry night. As Albers and James (1988) argue, image-based media—such as photographs, postcards, and posters—are not only the primary means to create and convey tourist destinations but also play a vital role in shaping tourist experiences. To better understand the rhetorical strategies tourist media use to construct the starry night, I will analyze one of the most prolific touristic campaigns for dark sky preserves, Tyler Nordgren's "Half the Park Is after Dark," a series of dark sky tourist posters promoting the U.S. National Park Service. While Nordgren's art style is as sublime and beautiful as the dark skies he wishes to promote, I will argue that ultimately his reliance on an outdated and ineffective form of sentimental nostalgia propagates an illusory and fantastical representation of dark skies that may not gain traction with the public. In other words, beauty won't save the starry night.

Half the Park Is after Dark

A professional astronomer, night sky ambassador, and visual artist, Tyler Nordgren illustrates how the fight to preserve darkness depends as much on the evocative power of art as it does on scientific outreach (Figure 5). In "Half the Park is After Dark," Nordgren blends a vintage esthetic style with breathtaking portrayals of the Milky Way, drawing inspiration from a century of romanticism that sees national parks as the last sanctuaries of untouched nature. Focusing on iconic landscapes such as the Grand Canyon and Mount Rainier, his posters reveal how these natural treasures come alive at night, offering astro-tourists a sublime escape to a nostalgic era unspoiled by urban light pollution.

Although public perceptions of national parks have shifted considerably since their inception in the early twentieth century (Demars, 1990), Nordgren's romanticized portrayal of the starry night reflects an outdated narrative that obscures the tangible threats facing the night sky. While the experience of sublime darkness can provide nocturnal visitors with awe-inspiring and profound encounters, it offers limited value as a conservation strategy, functioning more as a form of escapism than a meaningful call to address light pollution. Much like the constructed myth of "wilderness" (Cronon, 1995; Denevan, 1992) that has historically shaped perceptions of national parks, Nordgren frames pristine darkness as a spiritual sanctuary, positioning untouched nature as a remedy for the damage caused by pervasive artificial lighting.

Figure 5. "See Alaska Poster" (source: Tyler Nordgren, https://www.tylernordgren.com/milky-way-posters).

This perspective is understandable; anyone who has gazed at the vastness of the Milky Way can attest to the profound sense of wonder and humility evoked by the astronomical sublime. However, as an environmental strategy, romanticizing the notion of "untouched" nature proves inadequate. Nordgren's nostalgic depiction of the sublime, while evocative, fetishizes the ancient qualities of the starry night, distorting and de-historicizing the sky by framing it as an atemporal and empty reality without depth (Barthes, 1999). For example, rather than critically addressing the corporate-driven transformations of the night sky—such as the explosive growth of the small satellite industry—Nordgren's posters idealize dark sky parks as "unchanging" and "authentic" sanctuaries, positioned in stark opposition to the perceived artificiality of urban modernity.

Nature Parks and the Myth of the Pristine

For over a century, national parks have been celebrated for their restorative qualities, with picturesque and sublime landscapes offering health and emotional benefits to weary urban travelers (Patin, 2012; Ward, 2005). In the early nineteenth century, many moral reformers envisioned untouched wilderness as a remedy for the moral decay and perceived emptiness of urban life (Beauregard, 2002; Conn, 2014). While the rise of secular, industrial society brought material advancements, such as electric lighting, it also fostered widespread dissatisfaction with urban modernity's concept of progress. This discontent drove many to seek "authentic" experiences in nature, away from the perceived artificiality of the city.

To escape the spiritual void created by the daily grind of urban life, many sought refuge in America's rugged and "untouched" western frontier. In the late 1800s, the naturalist John Muir (2020) observed:

> Thousands of tired, nerve-shaken, over-civilized people are beginning to find out that going to the mountains is going home; that wildness is a necessity; and that mountain parks and reservations are useful not only as fountains of timber and irrigating rivers, but as fountains of life. Awakening from the stupefying effects of the vice of over-industry and the deadly apathy of luxury, they are trying as best they can to mix and enrich their own little ongoings with those of Nature, and to get rid of rust and disease.

Muir's anti-modernism was deeply rooted in the Romantic Movement, particularly the belief that close attention to nature offered moral benefits (Demars, 1990). For instance, the natural philosopher Emerson

(2019) praised rural landscapes for their power to counteract the moral failings of industrialization, suggesting that observing nature with "new eyes" allowed one to find manifestations of the divine. As he put it, "Our hunting for the picturesque is inseparable from our protest against false society" (39).

In his seminal critique of "wilderness," William Cronon (1995) explores the U.S. environmental movement's distinct approach to conserving pristine nature through the establishment of national parks. As urban life came to dominate American culture, Cronon argues, national parks became powerful symbols of ecological purity, perceived as vital sanctuaries for countering the spiritual decline associated with modernity. Mass tourism played a central role in legitimizing and sanctifying these landscapes, transforming parks such as Yellowstone, Yosemite, and Zion into sacred spaces distinct from the chaos of urban existence. Similarly, in his analysis of the Grand Canyon's enduring appeal, Mark Neumann (1999) notes:

> At the turn of this century, on the rim of its great empty chasm, a tourist world took shape that continually sought to affirm itself as a refuge from the modern world. More than anything, the Grand Canyon was a natural scene dramatizing how tourism and modernization went hand in hand. Historically, canyon tourists appear against a backdrop of broad cultural transformations that took hold of America in the last decades of the nineteenth century.

In this context, tourism did more than promoting these landscapes as escapes from urban life—it wove them into the larger cultural narrative of modernization, positioning nature as both a retreat and a reflection of the era's values.

The nineteenth-century belief that protected nature parks serve as a moral bulwark against urbanization persists in contemporary promotional materials for dark sky parks and preserves. Much like earlier travel guidebooks, brochures, and magazine articles that urged the public to experience the sublime beauty of protected landscapes, Nordgren's "Half the Park Is after Dark" frames the astro-tourist as a modern nocturnal explorer, seeking refuge in pristine darkness to escape the monotony of urban life. For example, in the poster for Alaska's Denali National Park and Preserve, an adventurous couple gazes up at the northern lights above a rugged mountain range, accompanied by the caption "Far from city lights, dark skies save the northern lights!" The message is clear: only the national park system can protect the night from the growing threat of urban light pollution. This theme runs consistently throughout the series. Nordgren's homage to the stewardship mission of the National Park Service exemplifies a continuation of nineteenth-century conservation ideals, heavily influenced by two Romantic tropes: the sublime wonder of nature and a nostalgic longing for the untamed frontier (Cronon, 1995).

From their inception, U.S. nature parks have drawn upon Romantic ideals of sublime wonder to elevate public awareness about the moral and spiritual value of untamed wilderness. Nordgren's images, rooted in the iconic settings of well-known national parks, inherit this Romantic legacy. Yet, as the series title "Half the Park Is after Dark" implies, an even more awe-inspiring vision of the park comes alive after sunset. When night falls and the Milky Way unfurls above the park's dramatic geological features, the viewer is invited to encounter a profound ancient marvel—the astronomical sublime (Figure 6). In many of the posters, Nordgren associates the astronomical sublime with the Milky Way, often portraying it as a cathedral of calm for a reflective, mature couple who stand serenely beneath the ancient stars. The blue immensity of the night sky appears to transport them to a time before modernity, evoking a primordial connection to the cosmos. These scenes resonate with Henry Van Dyke's (2005) notion of "wordless worship," a state of quiet reverence in which the vast silence of the universe fosters a deep, enduring bond between humanity and nature.

While geological examples of the sublime typically evoke the overwhelming power of earthbound nature—such as the sheer scale of mountains or the force of raging rivers—the astronomical sublime reaches even further. In Nordgren's posters, gazing upward at the Milky Way opens a window into the deeper meaning of the cosmos, echoing the romantic sensibility captured by Tennyson's (1987) night poet. "For the poet of the night sky [...] who looks up, not out," Tennyson observed, "the task is to totalize something that cannot be encompassed: the infinitude of the universe itself." This "sublime of awe," as Anne Janowitz (2005) describes it, emerged in the eighteenth century as the leading framework for contemplating the mysteries of the night sky, celebrating the triumphs of the human intellect in grasping the vastness of the universe. Nordgren explicitly draws on this tradition in his poster for the Arches International dark sky park, where the Milky Way is depicted as a shared resource that enhances the moral good of all humanity. The image features a striking scene of a solitary sandstone arch reaching toward the Milky Way, accompanied by the caption: "Windows to the Universe." In another poster, the night sky's ancient unifying power is emphasized. A pastoral image of the Milky Way is paired with a quote from John Muir: "We all travel the Milky Way, trees and men," suggesting that the cosmic experience connects all living things across time and space.

Notably absent from Nordgren's depiction of the astronomical sublime is any acknowledgment of the potential terrors inherent in confronting

Figure 6. The astronomical sublime (source: Tyler Nordgren, https://www.tylernordgren.com/milky-way-posters).

the "abyss" of nature. This more unsettling dimension of the sublime was articulated by Edmund Burke in 1757 when he discussed the fear and vulnerability that darkness can evoke:

> For in utter darkness, it is impossible to know in what degree of safety we stand; we are ignorant of the objects that surround us; we may every moment strike against some dangerous obstruction; we may fall down a precipice the first step we take; and if any enemy approach, we know not in what quarter to defend ourselves; in such a case strength is no sure protection; wisdom can only act by guess; the boldest are staggered, and he who would pray for nothing else towards his defence, is forced to pray for light.

In contrast, Nordgren's portrayal of the sublime is sentimental, tranquil, and domesticated, as his nostalgic style effectively tames the wilder, more fearsome qualities of the night. This softened vision is achieved, in part, through the recurring depiction of a happy, upper-class, white family—the demographic most likely to visit national parks. For instance, in the Mayo Dark Sky Preserve poster, a white mother and child gaze at the Milky Way with wide-eyed wonder, presenting the night sky as a realm of playful innocence (Figure 7). Likewise, in other posters, the sublime is further tamed through the recurring image of a happy domestic couple standing in composed, quiet contemplation. Their calm posture and reflective silence evoke the "proper" spiritual attitudes traditionally associated with the Romantics' appreciation of nature's enchantment and mystery. This framing of the night reinforces a controlled and harmonious sense of awe, removing the chaotic or fear-inducing elements that Burke identified as integral to the sublime experience. According to Cronon, this domestication of the sublime was closely tied to the rise of the modern tourist industry. While urban travelers sought encounters with "wild" nature to rejuvenate their spirits, they expected these experiences to be comfortable and accommodating. Cronon explains:

> By the second half of the nineteenth century, the terrible awe that Wordsworth and Thoreau regarded as the appropriately pious stance to adopt in the presence of their mountaintop God was giving way to a much more comfortable, almost sentimental demeanor. As more and more tourists sought out the wilderness as a spectacle to be looked at and enjoyed for its great beauty, the sublime in effect became domesticated. The wilderness was still sacred, but the religious sentiments it evoked were more those of a pleasant parish church than those of a grand cathedral or a harsh desert retreat. (6)

Figure 7. "Mayo Dark Sky Park" (source: Tyler Nordgren, https://www.tylernordgren.com/milky-way-posters).

This touristic experience with sentimental nature marked a fundamental shift in how nature was experienced. No longer a realm of overwhelming, untamed awe, wilderness was reframed as a managed, esthetically curated environment—one that could inspire admiration while remaining accessible and nonthreatening to visitors.

In addition to using the astronomical sublime to attract tourists, Nordgren draws on another familiar romantic trope from twentieth-century conservation movements: frontier nostalgia. As Cronon observes, "Those who have celebrated the frontier have almost always looked backward as they did so, mourning an older, simpler, truer world that is about to disappear, forever" (7). The recent surge of public interest in reconnecting with dark skies is undoubtedly fueled by growing fears of their rapid disappearance. To combat this loss, many dark sky parks promote the value of darkness by appealing to what John Urry (1994) describes as "glacial time"—a form of nostalgia in which a place is made to appear as though it has resisted the encroachments of modernity. For Urry, the significance of glacial time lies not only in its ability to foster a deep connection between the tourist and human history but also in how it leads tourists to envision the past as something timeless and unchanging.

In "Half the Park Is after Dark," Nordgren calls upon the myth of the American frontier—a space traditionally associated with freedom and untamed openness that has long inspired the astronomical imagination—to craft his glacial vision of the starry night. Much like the Western pioneers in the frontier myth, who cast themselves as heroic figures reclaiming freedom from the constraints of civilization, Nordgren's reflective family is portrayed as heirs to a vanishing culture of adventurers. They appear to long for a nostalgic return to a preindustrial golden age, rather than confronting the modern ecological realities of what has been called the "ends of nature."

The irony in Nordgren's depiction of the starry night is unmistakable. Although dark sky parks and preserves are a contemporary tourism phenomenon—some having received certification only in recent years (Dunnett, 2015)—the astronomical scenes Nordgren depicts are strikingly dated. In stark contrast to the glaring artificiality of urban nights, his imagery features a nostalgic, time-traveling couple, whose rustic early nineteenth-century attire reinforces a romanticized vision of the past. For instance, the posters make no reference to the various optical technologies—digital cameras, high-powered telescopes, or star trackers—that contemporary astro-tourists commonly use to experience the starry night. Instead, Nordgren purifies the astronomical sublime by implying that the most authentic way to experience its beauty is with the naked eye. This anti-technological approach to the cosmos reinforces the park's portrayal as an ancient, unspoiled inheritance, free from the trappings of modern technology, and reconnecting visitors with a supposedly timeless past.

Beauty Won't Save the Starry Night

By capitalizing on the sublime wonders of pristine darkness, astro-tourism reverses a long-standing moral order: whereas rural places were often associated with decline and regression, today, possessing an uncontaminated view of the stars gives the countryside a moral advantage over the city's excessive illumination. But can beauty alone save the starry night? For many dark sky advocates, the answer is a resoundingly yes. As Terrel Gallaway (2010) writes, "[…] those who have never seen a night sky ablaze with stars will lack sufficient information to judge the magnitude of their loss" (79). For Gallaway, only "the passive enjoyment" of the night will help the public change its mind about the value of darkness. Economic incentives, energy efficiency, and other utilitarian policies might offer short-term solutions to the growing problems of light pollution. However, as Gallaway observes, "utility bills do not well reflect what is culturally special about dark skies—the beauty that is the night's true comparative advantage. It is hard to imagine, therefore, a long-term solution to light pollution that does not explicitly recognize the fundamental role natural beauty plays in social welfare" (81).

I do not doubt that a sky filled with countless stars holds esthetic appeal that could encourage people to "turn down the lights" and conserve darkness. Gallaway's assertion that neglecting the night's beauty is a conservationist mistake that we should avoid making, however, overlooks the fact that esthetics have long been the primary strategy for protecting "wild" nature, especially in the context of American environmentalism. Moreover, as I have demonstrated in this chapter, some of the most popular and striking promotional materials for dark sky tourist destinations do not merely highlight the night's beauty—they remain steeped in the rustic and rural ideals of a romantic tradition that holds little value for a contemporary society that is largely urban. Therefore, the notion that appealing solely to the natural beauty of the ancient night is the only way to ensure that its protection is a limited and narrow approach, one that risks obscuring the actual realities facing the decline of darkness.

The more relevant question, I believe, is not how we can increase public appreciation for the night's beauty, but rather, how does framing the night through romantic ideals hinder efforts to protect the starry sky? As William Cronon argues, the key lesson from the cultural baggage of "pristine wilderness" is that when environmental conservation is centered on the loss of beauty, it often perpetuates problematic ideas about nature that pose a "serious threat to responsible environmentalism" (12). Indeed, extensive ecological research (Holt, 2012) indicates that the conventional belief that environmental issues can be best addressed by replacing the consumer values of urban society with those rooted in unspoiled landscapes or premodern ideals is rarely effective. Instead of fostering genuine change, this approach risks reinforcing nostalgic and unrealistic views of nature that may undermine more pragmatic and inclusive conservation efforts.

From the very outset of the national park movement, the dangers of overrelying on the allure of beautiful places were voiced by many critics. For instance, American philosopher John Dewey (1999) critiqued the public's fascination with picturesque locations as a form of escapism, especially the way many people used mass tourism to avoid confronting the urgent issues of the industrial age. "Many American critics of the present scene are engaged in devising modes of escape," Dewey noted. "Some flee to Paris or Florence; others take flight in their imagination to India, Athens, the Middle Ages or the American age of Emerson, Thoreau, and Melville. Flight is solution by evasion" (101). While Dewey acknowledged the grace and charm of America's newly established national parks, he insisted that beauty alone was insufficient to address the significant problems caused by industrialization. As he put it, "There is no need to deny the grace and beauty of some of these constructions. But when their imaginary character is once made apparent, it is futile to suppose that men can go on living and sustaining life by them" (102). In these damning critiques, Dewey underscores the limitations of relying solely on esthetic appreciation to drive meaningful environmental action, cautioning against viewing beautiful landscapes as substitutes for real solutions to societal and ecological challenges.

Although Dewey's criticism was made in the early twentieth century, when mass travel was in its infancy, many of his observations about the problem of using idealized places to confront contemporary problems are just as apt today. Simone Abram (2003), for example, updates many of Dewey's concerns through her idea of the rural gaze, the idea that urbanites romanticize the countryside by idealizing the past through rustic and pastoral touristic images. Like Dewey, Abram is wary of how sentimental yearning for the picturesque conceals the inequalities, conflicts, and tensions facing rural peoples in the present. As she writes, "The tourist gaze upon the rural landscape is one and the same as the rural gaze that estheticizes land uses in a nostalgic way in an attempt to distance it from contemporary capital and globalizing processes" (35). Similarly, for Cronon, the problem with nature parks is that by defining "pristine" nature as that which lies beyond human intervention, conservationists create a series of binary divisions that erase history. "In virtually all of its manifestations," he writes:

> Wilderness represents a flight from history. Seen as the original garden, it is a place outside of time, from which human beings had to be ejected before the fallen world of history could properly begin. Seen as the frontier, it is a savage world at the dawn of civilization, whose transformation represents the very beginning of the national historical epic (10).

What Dewey, Abram, and Cronon all share in common is the belief that confronting contemporary problems, like urban light pollution, requires a mode of thinking free from the reactionary and oversimplified impulses of romantic nostalgia. Instead of enticing viewers with rare and majestic views of the night sky, it is more helpful to interrogate the myths that sustain the idea that "pristine" darkness provides moral fodder for restoring humanity's connection to the night. Nordgren's nostalgic and sublime account of the starry night is undoubtedly astonishing. However, his presentation of the night is neither natural nor authentic, but an act of rhetorical mythmaking, since what he chooses to show and not to show shapes how tourists experience and understand darkness. As Lawrence Prelli (2006) argues, "the rhetorical power of images resides as much in what they conceal as in what they put on display." "Whatever is revealed through display," Prelli observes, "simultaneously conceals alternative possibilities; therein is display's rhetorical dimension" (24).

One glaring problem concealed by Nordgren's construction of the astronomical sublime is the ongoing material transformations taking place in outer space. While the night sky could be seen as a wild, untouched frontier before the launch of Sputnik in 1957, the contemporary sky continues to be subject to various ongoing technological, political, and corporate expansion projects. According to Peter L. Hays (2015), we now live in a fourth stage of space power, a new space race wherein the elite extract wealth from new forms of space tourism and small satellites. However, despite the global reach of this new stage of colonial space power (some estimate that by 2030 the small satellite industry will block out the view of most stars), most citizens fail to notice the space infrastructure underpinning modern life. As Patrick McCray (2021) writes, "As I write [...], thousands of objects of varying size are orbiting the earth. Hundreds of these are functioning satellites. These objects girding the globe are critical links in a modern technological and scientific infrastructure that most people reflect on little, if not at all."

Ironically, it is the astro-tourist who is most attuned to the adverse effects that space expansion projects have on the night sky. Anyone who has attempted to photograph the night sky understands that satellite trails—those bright, thin

Figure 8. Satellite trails (source: Science, https://www.science.org/content/article/worst-nightmare-elon-musk-s-starlink-satellites-could-blind-radio-telescopes).

lines appearing in long-exposure images—are now an unavoidable visual and material feature of the contemporary night sky (Figure 8). Even the darkest, most secluded dark sky parks and preserves cannot escape this new form of light pollution. Yet, by promoting the idea that national parks provide an unspoiled connection to the wonders of the ancient night, Nordgren's posters contribute to what Nicholas Mirzoeff (2014) describes as "Anthropocene visuality," a way of perceiving environmental issues that "[…] allows us to move on, to see nothing […] " (217). The danger in clinging to the notion that the untainted night is our ancient home is that, as Cronon (1995) argues, "we give ourselves permission to evade responsibility for the lives we actually lead. We inhabit civilization while holding some part of ourselves—what we imagine to be the most precious part—aloof from its entanglements" (11). From this perspective, what the sublime night actually achieves is the promotion of a mythological version of unspoiled nature that fosters a disconnect between our actions and their impact on the environment, obscuring the urgent need to confront the technological and industrial factors that continue to alter the night sky.

Conclusion

A recent study published in *Science* (Mortillaro, 2023) analyzed data from the Globe at Night outreach program to assess the annual rate of light pollution, finding that global light output has increased by 7%–10% annually over the past twelve years. To put this loss into perspective, while a stargazer twelve years ago might have been able to see 250 stars, today that number would be reduced to just 100. Many dark sky advocates argue that the growing problem of light pollution can be addressed by appealing to the public's appreciation for beauty. However, when viewed through the lens of national park conservation history, the notion that beauty alone can save the night falls short. Like with other forms of ecotourism, the appeal to esthetics repeats the ideological limitations of the myth of "pristine" nature. By elevating "pristine" darkness as the ideal standard for what qualifies as naturally wondrous, we risk creating an unattainable benchmark that dismisses other, less pure experiences with darkness—such as everyday interactions with gloom—that could still inspire people to care about preserving the night. More troubling, however, is the romanticization of the night, which erases traces of modern life and represents a retreat from history. While appealing to esthetic sensibilities may succeed in fostering a sense of wonder for the night sky, it falls short in addressing the deeper, systemic challenges required to combat light pollution. By focusing on nostalgia and purity, this approach risks sidelining critical conversations about the socioeconomic and technological drivers behind the degradation of the night, ultimately limiting its effectiveness as a conservation strategy.

To preserve the starry night, what is needed is an alternative approach to observing the sky—one that acknowledges its beauty while also drawing attention to the technological infrastructures increasingly colonizing the night. A valuable model for such a practice can be found in the "Moonwatchers" collective from the first space age. Following the Soviet launch of *Sputnik*, this small group of citizen scientists took to the sky each night, searching for critical data about early satellites. Although their efforts emerged during an era of optimism about the benefits of space exploration—a faith in scientific progress that has since waned—their global initiative to bring visibility to new technological artifacts remains instructive. For if the task of the critic is to reveal the gap between the idealized and reality (Berger, 2008), then what the "Moonwatchers" showed is that despite the remoteness of outer space—a distance that has allowed for wild and troubling idealizations of the night sky—it is possible to bridge the divide between appreciating the night's esthetic appeal and recognizing the technological forces at play, offering a more nuanced and critical approach to engaging with the night sky that confronts both its beauty and transformation by human activities.

For those seeking to ground the hidden space infrastructure that contaminates the night, there are visual practices and precedents that astro-tourism can adopt. The space archaeology of Alice Gorman (2019) and the infrastructural media studies of Lisa Parks (2005), for instance, offer two prominent frameworks in which images of satellites serve as starting points for examining the power dynamics and inequalities linked to satellite technologies. By beginning with a "footprint" analysis of the sky, which prioritizes the material realities over the romantic sublime, both approaches emphasize that "the earth and the sky above are filled not just with the mysteries and magic of nature, but also with the complex interventions of humankind" (Pasternak and Thompson, 2012). Incorporating these perspectives into astro-tourism could transform its visual practices, allowing tourists not only to appreciate the beauty of the night sky but also to critically engage with the human-made structures impacting it.

Chapter Three

ERASING THE NIGHT SKY: SATELLITES, ASTROPHOTOGRAPHY, AND THE CONSTRUCTION OF VISUAL POLLUTION

Introduction

Every summer for the past eight years, I have traveled to Terra Nova National Park, a dark sky preserve located on the east coast of Newfoundland, to photograph the breathtaking Perseid meteor shower. This annual event, which is created by debris from the comet Swift-Tuttle, typically occurs between midJuly and late August. Since receiving its dark sky certification in 2018, Terra Nova has become a premier destination for observing the meteor shower, as it boasts some of the darkest skies in eastern North America. Yet, despite the park's dedicated efforts to preserve darkness, a growing challenge for visitors, especially astrophotographers, involves the proliferation of active and defunct orbiting satellites. Since satellites often leave "satellite trails"—streaks of light visible in long-exposure images that can easily be mistaken for shooting stars—many astrophotographers are unable to produce "pristine" images of the Milky Way. To mitigate these so-called visual pollutants, many photographers employ specialized software and advanced AI tools to digitally remove the intrusive satellite trails, restoring the night sky to its natural, unblemished beauty. Thus, unlike in Chapter Two, where it was shown how artists, like Tyler Nordgren, rely on nostalgia to preserve dark skies, in this chapter, I explore how advanced AI technologies are used to maintain the illusion of pristine celestial wonders despite the impacts of modern human activity in space.

While satellite trails may seem like a minor inconvenience for amateur astrophotographers, referring to them as a mere visual nuisance understates their broader implications. The rapid expansion of the internet satellite industry, driven by companies such as Starlink and OneWeb, has turned satellites and their debris into a significant but underreported environmental concern. Unlike high-profile issues such as the Anthropocene and climate change, which dominate discourse in the environmental humanities, and are the primary ecological issues used to critique unchecked capitalist growth, the environmental and scientific consequences of satellites and space debris often receive insufficient attention. This oversight is troubling. If left unchecked, some experts warn that by 2030, the proliferation of satellites could fundamentally alter our relationship with the night sky, making it increasingly difficult to enjoy views of many celestial phenomena. More critically, this growth threatens essential ground-based astronomical practices, including observational research and asteroid detection systems crucial for planetary defense. Without greater awareness and intervention, the unchecked expansion of the satellite industry risks not only obscuring humanity's shared heritage of the night sky but also undermining vital scientific tools needed to protect life on Earth.

In this chapter, I analyze two contrasting media representations of satellites to explore how contemporary media can either obscure or illuminate the political implications of space debris and the challenges posed by the rapidly expanding satellite internet industry. While recent scholarship in the environmental humanities has begun to address the political, social, and ecological dimensions of waste and obsolescence, media studies have largely neglected the visual politics of space pollution. For instance, while the long-term challenges posed by plastics are widely recognized, fewer people are aware that satellite technology generates enduring waste that may persist far beyond human civilization. Operating in a near-zero gravitational environment, satellites deteriorate much more slowly than objects on Earth. As a result, they function as an "eternal" technology, continuing to orbit long after their utility has ended. This disjunction between the accelerated pace of global capitalist societies, which prioritize speed and obsolescence, and the protracted lifespans of technologies designed to endure indefinitely, represents a critical ecological challenge of our time. In this chapter, I aim to shed light on the overlooked issue of space pollution, emphasizing the necessity of resisting neoliberal narratives that frame outer space as a site for unlimited exploitation. Through this lens, I critique the tendency to regard the night sky as a politically neutral realm of sublime beauty, arguing that artists and media practitioners can play a vital role in challenging these assumptions and drawing attention to the complex political and environmental stakes of space exploration and satellite technology.

The Race to Space: Media Empires and Neoliberalism

On May 23, 2019, SpaceX launched its first batch of 60 Starlink satellites from Cape Canaveral Air Force Station in Florida, marking the beginning of Elon Musk's ambitious initiative to deliver high-speed internet access to underserved remote and rural regions around the globe. Musk's endeavor represents a significant step forward in addressing the spatial inequalities and uneven development characteristic of global capitalist societies. Contrary to the idealized notion of a "network society," where citizens are seamlessly integrated into a vast, interconnected web through advanced technologies, the reality is that connectivity often remains concentrated in urban centers. Many rural and remote areas exist on the margins of these networks, frequently grappling with limited or entirely absent internet access. Even in regions where some level of connectivity exists, slow and unreliable bandwidth restricts meaningful participation in digital society and reinforces existing inequalities. While the Starlink project aims to bridge this digital divide, offering a technological solution to a deeply entrenched issue of global inequity, this effort also raises questions about the environmental, social, and political implications of relying on satellite infrastructure to resolve complex problems of access and development.

Despite the media fascination with Elon Musk's grand plans for Mars colonization, there has been surprisingly little scrutiny of his monopolistic dominance over the satellite internet industry. Since 2019, Starlink has launched over 6,000 satellites into orbit, establishing Musk as a central figure in the satellite broadband market. This quiet but rapid consolidation of power highlights the deep structural imbalances within global media industries, where a few influential players shape the future of connectivity and space exploration. James Hay's (2020) analysis of space power provides a valuable lens through which to understand this phenomenon.

Hays argues that the emergence of neoliberal global societies in the 1990s marked a new phase of space warfare, characterized by competing media empires vying for control over the satellite broadband spectrum. During this time, outer space began to be framed as a capitalist frontier, evoking comparisons to the Wild West—a vast, unregulated expanse ripe for conquest and exploitation through neoliberal policies and market competition. Musk's seamless positioning as a leader in the privatization and colonization of outer space exemplifies this legacy. His dominance reflects not only the technological and economic shifts of the satellite industry but also broader ideological trends that equate technological innovation with progress, while sidelining critical discussions about environmental, social, and political equity in space. Like other forms of neoliberalism, Musk perpetuates a vision of space as an extension of Earth's capitalist systems, reinforcing existing inequalities, and prioritizing profit over collective stewardship of the night sky.

Erasing the Night Sky: Satellites and the De-Politicization of Outer Space

One of the most pressing challenges posed by the neoliberal governance of space is the unchecked deployment of satellites and the absence of robust regulations to address the resulting accumulation of space debris and waste. For example, SpaceX's inaugural Starlink launch is widely regarded by professional astronomers as a dangerous turning point where the sharp increase in small satellite deployments threatens to significantly compromise ground-based astronomical observations. Despite some efforts by SpaceX to collaborate with astronomers and mitigate the impact of its satellites, such as reducing their reflectivity, the astronomical community was caught off guard by the extent of light pollution they produced. The satellites' reflective surfaces, for instance, were far brighter than anticipated, interfering with long-exposure imaging and other observational practices. Compounding the issue, many astronomers were unaware of the small satellite industry's plans to launch over 100,000 satellites within the next two decades—a figure that would drastically alter the night sky.

With minimal regulatory oversight to constrain the rapid growth of the satellite industry, the future of ground-based astronomy appears increasingly precarious. As light pollution from satellites intensifies, clear and unobstructed views of the cosmos—an essential component of astronomical research—are becoming ever more elusive. Without coordinated global action to address this issue, the cumulative effects of satellite proliferation and space debris will fundamentally reshape humanity's relationship with the night sky, potentially closing a chapter of discovery that has defined scientific inquiry for centuries.

In response to these alarming developments, the American Astronomical Society (AAS) convened a virtual workshop to assess the potential impacts of Low Earth Orbit satellites on the astronomical community and beyond. The workshop highlighted a range of potential disruptions for professional astronomers, including compromised asteroid detection systems and inaccurate photometric readings, as well as the broader effects of unchecked light pollution on the general public's ability to stargaze and experience the night sky. Drawing on rhetorical strategies often employed by environmental preservationists, participants characterized the proliferation of satellites as an unprecedented form of visual pollution. They described the satellites as defiling, polluting, and tarnishing the ancestral legacy of unspoiled night skies, emphasizing the profound cultural and scientific significance of preserving this natural resource. Jeffrey Hall (EarthSky Voices, 2019), Chair of the AAS Committee on Light Pollution, Radio Interference, and Space Debris, underscored the gravity of the issue, stating, "The natural night sky is a resource not just for astronomers, but for all who look upward to understand and enjoy the splendor of the universe, and its degradation has far-reaching negative impacts that extend beyond the realm of astronomy." Throughout the report, the problem of satellite light pollution is framed as not merely a technical challenge for scientists, but a broader cultural and environmental issue with implications for humanity's shared connection to the cosmos. By linking the preservation of the night sky to both scientific inquiry and public enjoyment, the workshop sought to galvanize support for more robust regulations and collective action to address the satellite industry's rapid and largely unregulated expansion.

To address the challenges posed by satellite light pollution, the workshop introduced SATCON1 (Walker et al., 2020), a document outlining various mitigation strategies. These range from the highly improbable suggestion of halting all future satellite launches to more actionable proposals, such as engineering satellites with lower reflectivity to minimize solar light reflection. However, one proposal stands out as emblematic of how neoliberal frameworks often undermine meaningful public engagement with urgent issues: the application of artificial intelligence. According to the SATCON1 report, a key concern for the astronomical community is OneWeb, a British company planning to deploy a substantial constellation of satellites in orbital ranges around 1,200 km above the Earth. Unlike SpaceX's satellites, which orbit at approximately 600 km and are visible mainly during twilight hours, higher-altitude satellites will pose a more severe threat to observations. Remaining visible throughout the night during summer months, these satellites will exacerbate the problem of satellite trails—bright, thin streaks captured in long-exposure astronomical images—that compromise the integrity of wide-field views of celestial phenomena like the Milky Way. To counteract this problem, the workshop proposed the development of a software application designed for the broader astronomy community. This tool would enable users to detect, simulate, remove, and obscure satellite trails in their images using customizable parameters. While practical, this solution underscores the paradoxical nature of modern efforts to preserve the night sky: to maintain the illusion of its pristine beauty, users must rely on digital interventions to erase all visible traces of satellite technology. In effect, stargazers are tasked with digitally altering the cosmos, masking the impacts of the very systems designed to deliver global connectivity. This approach reveals a troubling tendency to shift the burden of mitigating environmental degradation from industry to individuals, perpetuating a cycle of reactive solutions rather than addressing the root causes of the issue.

My critique of these software solutions is not intended to diminish their scientific value. On the contrary, digitally removing satellite trails is a crucial tool for professional astronomers, enabling the preservation of observational data and helping mitigate the growing risks of light pollution. However, I argue that from an aesthetic and representational standpoint, these post-processing techniques may ultimately do more harm than good. If organizations such as the American Astronomical Society (AAS) and the International Dark-Sky Association are committed to raising public awareness about the degradation of the night sky and ensuring that future generations can experience its beauty, digitally erasing satellite trails risks undermining these efforts. Such practices could contribute to what Nicholas Mirzoeff (2014) terms "Anthropocene Visuality"—an image-making approach that obscures the material realities and environmental consequences of human activity. By "cleaning up" the visual evidence of satellite pollution, these techniques may unintentionally perpetuate a false perception of the cosmos as unspoiled and eternal, masking the pressing environmental issues that threaten it.

To explore the implications of these post-processing strategies, I will analyze the aesthetic and representational conventions employed in astrophotography to frame satellite trails as visual pollutants. By doing so, I aim to highlight how these conventions influence public understanding of light pollution and the environmental challenges posed by the rapid expansion of satellite technology.

Light Trails as Visual Pollutants

In environmental studies, remediation refers to the process of removing toxic contaminants or pollutants from an ecosystem, with the goal of restoring its health and functionality. This process of restoration relies on a combination of regulatory frameworks and technological interventions to address environmental damage. However, even after remediation is deemed successful, the ecosystem does not return to a pre-impact state of untouched nature. Instead, it forms a hybrid condition—one that continues to bear the imprint of human influence. This ongoing need for human oversight underscores a fundamental paradox helpful in addressing the problem of seeking pristine dark skies: while remediation seeks to heal ecosystems from human activity, it also necessitates sustained human intervention to ensure the environment remains free of contaminants. Thus, the concept of remediation highlights the impossibility of truly "pristine" nature in the Anthropocene. Unlike many environmentalists, who claim that the solution to ecological troubles involves human detachments from nature, what remediation shows is that environmental protection requires more human activity not less to ensure "healthy" relationships between humans and the natural world (Latour, 2012).

In the field of media studies, the concept of environmental remediation aligns closely with Richard Grusin's (2004) theory of how mass media remediates nature, a process shaped by the interplay of two opposing media logics. On one hand, remediation involves the deployment of transparent representational techniques designed to conceal or minimize the technological and human processes of representation. This approach produces idealized depictions of nature as a pristine, unspoiled paradise, seemingly untouched by human influence. Much like the physical removal of contaminants during environmental remediation, visual media often "cleanses" the nature of any visible traces of human or technological intervention, presenting it as an eternal and untouched wilderness.

A prime example of this media logic is Disney's True-Life Adventures documentaries, which adopted a highly polished visual style to depict nature as a "wild frontier" of vast, untouched landscapes. These films strategically exclude evidence of cameras, crew, and other human activity, reinforcing a preservationist perspective that idealizes nature as separate from humanity. This framing not only perpetuates the myth of "untouched" wilderness but also obscures the complex, ongoing interactions between human activity and the environment. By erasing these connections, media representations risk creating a nostalgic and static vision of nature that undermines a nuanced understanding of ecological interdependence in the Anthropocene.

Conversely, the effort to erase and conceal human and technological elements in media representations often results in hypermediacy—a condition where media proliferation paradoxically heightens awareness of the technological intermediaries required to create the illusion of unmediated access to nature. This dynamic is exemplified by virtual reality (VR) technology, which offers fully immersive 360-degree experiences of "breathtaking" natural landscapes. For users, the sensation of "being present" within these environments can evoke profound emotional connections to nature, fostering awe, and appreciation. However, this immersive experience depends on navigating a range of technological interfaces, such as bulky VR headsets, restrictive cables, and carefully calibrated software. These tools, while designed to vanish into the background, often become acutely noticeable due to their physicality and complexity. The resulting tension between the immersive illusion and the conspicuous mediation illustrates the paradox of the media: while striving to present an idealized, direct connection to nature, the medium simultaneously underscores the layers of technological intervention necessary to sustain the experience. This duality reflects a broader pattern in media remediation, where attempts to conceal human influence often expose the very technologies and processes they aim to obscure.

Grusin's concept of remediation provides a lens through which we can understand how astrophotography not only frames satellite trails as visual pollutants but also employs post-processing techniques to depoliticize the infrastructure occupying outer space. Like nature parks and traditional landscape painting, astrophotography is an art form rooted in the aesthetic of concealment. To achieve cultural recognition, astrophotographers often draw on the traditions of nineteenth-century landscape art, employing wide-angle, panoramic compositions to immerse viewers in the grandeur and sublimity of the cosmos (Kessler, 2012). As Kessler writes, in a time when environmentalists caution against the crisis of overdevelopment, the night sky is often conceptualized as humanity's last unspoiled frontier—a sanctuary of uncorrupted wilderness where individuals can reconnect with a shared natural heritage that spans human history. By digitally erasing satellite trails, astrophotography perpetuates a long-standing tradition of depicting nature as an idealized, pristine realm, untouched by technological progress. While aesthetically powerful, this practice risks obscuring the material realities of space infrastructure and its environmental consequences, reinforcing a romanticized vision of the cosmos that aligns with preservationist ideals while sidestepping the political and ecological complexities of the Anthropocene.

Indeed, while the astronomical community often emphasizes the importance of deep time and the ancestral heritage of dark skies, it rarely critiques how this pursuit of purity reinforces a normative view of "civilization" as an inherently polluting force that must be excised from nature. Mary Douglas, in her seminal work on dirt and purity, provides a useful framework for understanding this dynamic. Douglas argues that pollution is not an intrinsic quality of matter but arises when something is perceived to be "out of place." As she writes, "Dirt is the byproduct of a systematic ordering and classification of matter, in so far as ordering involves rejecting inappropriate elements" (2002, 44). In this context, satellite trails—artifacts of modern technology—represent "misplaced" elements in the ancestral night sky. Unlike the bright streaks of light produced by asteroids or comets, which are celebrated as natural phenomena and awe-inspiring wonders, satellite trails are classified as unwelcome visual pollutants. As such, they disrupt the romanticized ideal of the cosmos as a pristine, unspoiled realm and must be digitally removed to preserve the illusion of purity. This distinction underscores the culturally constructed nature of pollution, whereby astrophotographers endorse a systematic privileging of certain forms of light and motion as "natural" while rejecting others as "technological intrusions," perpetuating a binary view of nature and civilization that can obscure the complex entanglements of human activity and the environment.

In addition to being the product of matter out of place, pollution also emerges through the measurement and narration of time. How things endure or run out of time also generates waste. As William Viney (2015) writes, "[…] using and discarding objects generates and maintains certain temporal relations, relations that help us organize our experience of the world. The obsolescence of use demonstrates something of the two-fold temporal quality of material things, that is, that the passing of utility both makes and marks time, that objects are produced by and productive of specific temporal relations." Crucially for Viney is the idea that the "passing of utility" is not a fixed, quantitative process. Objects do not inherently possess a set duration of use-value that runs out of time; rather, their use-value is culturally and socially constructed through narratives.

Within the astronomical community, satellites are prime examples of this duality. From one perspective, they are highly functional objects with abundant use-value, enabling global internet connectivity and facilitating the dissemination of astronomical knowledge. Satellites make it possible to share stunning images of the cosmos across social networks and provide platforms for collaborative scientific engagement. However, when viewed through the lens of "pristine nature" satellites transform into unwelcome detritus. Despite their technological utility, they disrupt the aesthetic and cultural narrative of an untouched cosmos. This dual framing illustrates how cultural narratives dictate the perceived value or pollution of objects: satellites are celebrated as enablers of connectivity and progress in one context while condemned as visual pollutants in another.

This contradiction—the way technology with significant use-value can simultaneously be regarded as unwelcome waste—can be better understood through Viney's exploration of an older concept of waste, one linked to temporal disorientation. Waste, in this framework, is not merely defined by the absence of utility but also by its freedom from human temporality. Viney notes that the Latin root of "waste," vastus, denotes an immense, uninhabited, wild space—something excessive and beyond practical human use. As Viney writes, "Put another way, waste is a condition of that which does not coincide with the time of human activity."

Astrophotography's celebration of "deep time" provides an excellent way to consider this perspective. Deep time refers to the immeasurable stretches of time and space that existed long before human life, positioning the night sky as a pristine, ancient expanse untouched by human influence. In Viney's terms, deep time itself can be seen as a kind of wasteland—a temporal and spatial place beyond human reach and practical value. Since many astrophotographers frame their images of the cosmos through the idea of deep time, satellites, which embody human technological progress and utility, appear as temporal misfits, their trails disrupting the aesthetic and symbolic coherence of a visual narrative that prioritizes timelessness and primordial purity. It is this misalignment—satellites being "out of place" because they are "out of time"—that renders them as contaminants. By invoking the "wrong" time, satellites challenge astrophotography's vision of the night sky as a sanctuary of untouched natural heritage. Thus, as visual pollutants, satellite trails and their digital erasure highlight a fundamental tension in astrophotography: the desire to preserve the timeless beauty of the cosmos requires the obfuscation of present realities, a process of remediation that complicates our understanding of nature, time, and human activity in the Anthropocene.

While the nostalgic allure of a night sky unencumbered by the neoliberal imperatives of capital is understandable, this portrayal of satellite pollution overlooks the profound transformations that have shaped outer space over the past several decades. Before the launch of Sputnik in 1957, outer space was often romanticized as a wild, unspoiled frontier, seemingly untouched by human influence. However, since the dawn of the space age, outer space has been subject to continuous technological, political, and corporate expansion efforts. The notion that outer space is a moral vacuum or an empty vessel awaiting human conquest, thus, fails to account for its complex history as a contested and instrumentalized space of technological development. For instance, during the Cold War, space became a stage for national prestige and geopolitical rivalry, with superpowers racing to demonstrate their technological and ideological dominance. By the 1990s, the dynamics of space power shifted, reflecting the rise of global telecommunications and the proliferation of cyber powers. In this neo-liberal climate, outer space became a crucial infrastructure for the global economy, facilitating everything from satellite communications to GPS navigation and internet connectivity. What this historical trajectory demonstrates is that outer space is neither untouched nor neutral—it is an actively constructed and deeply politicized place shaped by competing national, corporate, and technological agendas. Depicting the night sky as a pristine, wilderness risks erasing this complex and contentious history, perpetuating a myth of purity that overlooks the ongoing imperialistic transformations taking place in outer space.

As Peter L. Hays observes, we are now living in a new stage of space power, characterized by the oligopolistic pursuits of private enterprises and global communications superpowers. Unlike the first space age, which was defined by the geopolitical and technological ambitions of Cold War rivalries, this new phase of space power is driven by the brazen ambitions of a select group of ultra-wealthy actors seeking to extract resources from outer space and capitalize on its economic potential. Furthermore, at the forefront of this new space race is the daily proliferation of satellite launches, a new technological routine that largely goes unnoticed by the public (Fernholz, 2018). As Patrick McCray notes, the initial wonder and excitement exemplified by the launch of Sputnik in 1957 has dissipated and been replaced by an infrastructural landscape that operates unseen in the background. "The novelty of what flashed and beeped in the October sky in 1957," McCray reflects, "is hard to appreciate today. As I write this, thousands of objects of varying sizes are orbiting the Earth. Hundreds of these are functioning satellites. These objects circling the globe are essential components of a modern technological and scientific framework that most people rarely consider, if at all."

This normalization of satellite infrastructure underscores a key distinction between the first space age and the current space race. While the early space age captivated citizen scientists and amateur observers, encouraging them to look skyward in awe, in today's space age, the everyday realities of outer space exploration remain invisible to the general public. Satellites, an essential component of modern life—facilitating global communication, surveillance, and navigation, are largely taken for granted. Their ubiquity, however, raises critical questions about how this unnoticed infrastructure shapes our relationship with outer space, redefining it as a commodified and industrialized domain under the purview of wealthy elites.

The lack of citizen involvement in the most recent race to space is why the AAA's endorsement of digitally erasing satellite trails is so troubling: in its pursuit of scientific clarity, it inadvertently fosters ignorance about both the impact of satellite technology on astronomy and the broader political question of who owns and has the right to experience the night sky. In this way, the erasure of the night sky contributes to the normalization of pollution through aesthetics. According to Mirzoeff, the dominant approach to representing environmental harm involves aestheticizing pollution by rendering it a tolerable, even beautiful, byproduct of modern life. This aesthetic framing reinforces the normative idea that environmental destruction is an unavoidable aspect of progress, while also downplaying its urgency. As Mirzoeff writes,

> Anthropocene visuality allows us to move on, to see nothing and keep circulating commodities, despite the destruction of the biosphere. We do so less out of venal convenience, as some might suggest, than out of a modernist conviction that 'the authorities' will restore everything to order in the end. In short, Anthropocene visuality keeps us believing that somehow the war against nature that Western society has been waging for centuries is not only right; it is beautiful and it can be won.

This aestheticized perspective, Mirzoeff argues, perpetuates the belief that the west's ongoing "war against nature" is not only justifiable but ultimately winnable. By removing visible traces of satellite pollution, astrophotographers risk contributing to this framework, treating the harm inflicted on the night sky as something manageable and secondary, rather than a pressing issue requiring systemic change.

In response to this way of visualizing the Anthropocene, Mirzoeff (2011) suggests that we search for a counter-visuality—an alternative way of seeing and representing environmental damage—that brings harm to the forefront of our daily lives. Like oil rigs and platforms, satellites operate in remote, inaccessible spaces, making them difficult to incorporate into public consciousness. Satellites, however, present an even greater challenge: their location in outer space restricts their visibility, leaving their presence to be understood only through mediated representations. As Elizabeth M. DeLoughrey (2014) observes, "Because extraterritorial spaces cannot be fully inhabited, we rely on their visual, specifically photographic representations by satellite and other vessels, to produce one of many scopic regimes of modernity." In the remainder of this chapter, I will explore how art can play a critical role in addressing these issues by making the invisible consequences of satellite technology visible and tangible. Through diverse artistic mediums—such as installations, visual art, and multimedia projects—artists can craft compelling narratives that challenge audiences to engage with the ethical, environmental, and cultural dilemmas satellites present. Specifically, I will explore two installations by Trevor Paglen, whose multimedia projects juxtapose satellite imagery with narratives of ecological disruption, highlighting the unintended consequences of technological advancements on Earth and beyond. Indeed, by blending aesthetics with activism, Paglen's artistic interventions become a mode of counter-visuality, challenging dominant narratives of progress and purity while emphasizing the interconnectedness of technology, environment, and humanity.

The Last Pictures

In recent years, University of Central Florida student Jack Sweeney has garnered widespread attention for tracking and publicly sharing the flight paths of private jets owned by high-profile celebrities such as Elon Musk and Taylor Swift. Sweeney's initiative has sparked heated debates online over the balance between public accountability and individual privacy. Critics, including Musk, argue that revealing this information compromises personal safety and privacy. Musk has even gone so far as to label the practice a security threat. In contrast, Sweeney defends his work as a legal and vital act of democratic engagement. By making flight data publicly accessible, his efforts highlight the environmental implications of private air travel, particularly the outsized carbon emissions associated with the ultra-wealthy. Indeed, viewed from the perspective of Mirzoeff's theories, Sweeney's work can be seen as a form of counter-visibility, his data serving to promote public dialogue around the often-hidden issue of environmental accountability and the need to push for greater scrutiny of the privileged lifestyles that contribute disproportionately to the global climate crisis.

While Trevor Paglen's work has not achieved the viral notoriety of Jack Sweeney's flight-tracking efforts, his installations similarly perform a vital public service by cultivating a politics of visibility that brings the often-invisible infrastructure of modern life into focus. Although many people have a general understanding of how satellite technology facilitates global data exchanges, comprehending the physicality and precise locations of these systems is far less intuitive. Paglen's art bridges this gap by persistently encouraging audiences to look upward and acknowledge the orbital technology that underpins contemporary information systems. As such, Paglen's projects resonate with Keller Easterling's (2014) concept of infrastructural space—the hidden power structures embedded in today's vast interconnected information networks and the large-scale architectural frameworks that make global communications possible.

According to Easterling, contemporary cities are increasingly shaped by large architectural systems that extend beyond physical structures to encompass the vast informational networks driving urban life. Among these systems, server networks supporting artificial intelligence and digital distribution channels are pivotal, silently managing the hidden patterns that sustain modern urbanity. Satellites are integral to this infrastructure as well, enabling a wide array of invisible information exchanges—from communication and navigation to surveillance and weather forecasting—essential for society's daily functioning. Yet, their position in outer space makes satellites difficult to detect and comprehend as part of the urban fabric. Unlike the landmark engineering feats of modernity, such as the railway system, which visibly reinforced state power and authority, satellites signify a new era of infrastructural design. Their immense architectural significance resides less in their architectural size and scale than in their near invisibility, a quality reinforced by the inaccessibility of orbital space. This feature of satellite technology makes them exemplary participants in the neoliberal logic of seamless global exchange, where technology appears to operate without disruption or resistance.

As an artist, whose work often zooms in on satellite technologies, Paglen challenges viewers to reconsider their relationship with infrastructural space, prompting greater awareness of the systems and structures that are typically taken for granted. For instance, one of the most striking examples of how his works bring visibility to hidden infrastructures is *The Last Pictures*, a 2012 art installation that transcends the traditional art gallery. Unlike artworks typically displayed in museums, *The Last Pictures* resides in the Clarke Belt—a geostationary orbit (GSO) that hosts thousands of satellites integral to modern communication. While most people are unaware of the Clarke Belt's significance, it forms a pivotal global media geography, which enables the rapid, near-instantaneous transmission of data that defines contemporary life. Satellites in this orbit power everything from social media updates and viral selfies to critical media systems like cellular coverage, television broadcasts, credit card transactions, and weather forecasts. The Clarke Belt is an especially prevalent orbital space for the production and dissemination of contemporary imagery. While major media conglomerates, like Facebook already contribute to the production and dissemination of billions of images annually—primarily transmitted through ground-based cable networks—the rise of small internet satellites is expanding the quantity of visual data that underpins image-based social systems in the West. For example, in addition to proliferating the countless images posted on social media platforms, the Clark Belt is home to a new generation of commercial satellites designed to capture high-resolution photographs of the Earth's entire landmass daily. Although some of this data is used for scientific purposes, such as tracking long-term weather patterns, much of it is commodified and sold to private surveillance firms, revealing a darker dimension of the satellite-driven economy.

To draw attention to the way contemporary media technologies are connected to this vital orbital space, Paglen created a gold-plated aluminum disc, containing 100 curated social media images, and affixed it to the Echostar XVI, a communications satellite designed to broadcast television signals. Nestled among satellites that underpin the digital infrastructure of daily life, *The Last Pictures* invites reflection on humanity's technological footprint in space. Engineered to endure for billions of years in the absence of gravity and atmospheric decay, the silicon-etched images evoke a concept of temporal endurance that contrasts sharply with the ephemerality of modern technological systems. Indeed, in contrast to the AAA's proposal to mitigate the prevalence of space debris by erasing it from view and restoring an illusory night sky of premodern wonder, Paglen's exposes the Clarke Belt's status as a highly contested neoliberal space defined by intense competition, surveillance, and the consolidation of power. Thus, by revealing the tension between the fleeting visual culture facilitated by satellites and their enduring physical presence in orbital space, *The Last Pictures* challenges the perception of satellites as ephemeral elements of modernity. Instead, the installation positions them as enduring artifacts of a neoliberal system that exploits invisibility to assert control (Figure 9).

Another significant project by Trevor Paglen that invites the public to reflect on the orbiting technology integral to contemporary societies is *Orbital Reflector*, a sculptural satellite launched in 2018. As the first satellite sent into orbit without a commercial, scientific, or military purpose, *Orbital Reflector* reflects Paglen's commitment to politicizing satellites by making them visible and engaging art objects. However, unlike the more inaccessible nature of *The Last Pictures* (after the launch, it proved challenging for the average person to

Figure 9. Golden Disc (source: Trevor Paglen, https://paglen.studio/2020/01/21/the-last-pictures/).

track the satellite), *Orbital Reflector* was designed to be seen with the naked eye, provided one knows where to look (Figure 10). This non-functional satellite, which was sent into low Earth orbit aboard a SpaceX rocket, is made of a highly reflective, lightweight material resembling Mylar. It was conceived to unfold into a bright, visible object in the night sky, offering viewers a moment to appreciate both the beauty of the cosmos and the evolving relationship between humanity and outer space.

However, as of 2025, the artwork remains encased in its CubeSat, a box-like structure used to house satellites before deployment. Due to delays in receiving clearance from the U.S. government, the satellite has yet to deploy, and there is no indication that it ever will. This situation leaves the fate of the project in limbo, highlighting the entanglement of space exploration with systems of governance that prioritize commercialization and militarization over cultural or public interests. As a stalled art project, *Orbital Reflector* becomes a poignant symbol of the ways outer space is constrained by institutional powers that regulate who controls and determines the fate of our planetary commons. Indeed, by orbiting Earth within a box unlikely to open, *Orbital Reflector* serves as a striking reminder that outer space is far from a neutral frontier. Instead, it is shaped by political and commercial forces that often obscure the infrastructure governing our social and technological lives. Thus, through projects, like *Orbital Reflector,* which bring satellite technologies

Figure 10. Mosaic of included images (source: Trevor Paglen, https://paglen.studio/2020/01/21/the-last-pictures/).

back down to earth, Paglen can raise critical questions about the invisibility of satellite technology and its ease of disappearance from public consciousness. More importantly, by blending aesthetics with the material realities of outer space, Paglen also urges us to consider not just the presence of satellites but their relationship to the incompatible timescales created by capitalism. That is, as media objects that will endure long after their use, satellites belong to a new category of monumental systems of technological waste.

Media Obsolescence

Will Straw's (2004) exploration of obsolescence provides an insightful framework for understanding how space debris is culturally constructed through the interaction of two distinct systems of decay. On the one hand, media obsolescence involves symbolic or semiotic decay, the process by which certain objects lose their aesthetic value or functional relevance due to shifts in cultural preferences or trends. For example, items like MP3 players or specific fashion accessories can become unfashionable, relegating them to irrelevance as cultural artifacts. The second system, physical decay, pertains to the inevitable material degradation of objects over time, regardless of their social or symbolic status. Straw argues that waste emerges from the interplay between these two forms of decay. An object deemed obsolete in one context may still retain value in another. For instance, while analog records were once overshadowed by newer digital technologies, their enduring functionality and cultural revaluation have allowed them to reemerge as symbols of retro sophistication or hipster prestige. This duality underscores how obsolescence is not an inherent property of objects but is instead shaped by cultural narratives and material realities. In capitalist systems, obsolescence is accelerated by the transient nature of consumer preferences. Durable and functional objects are often discarded prematurely to make way for newer, trendier commodities. This cycle of consumption produces waste that is simultaneously cultural and material, reflecting the broader dynamics of a system that prioritizes novelty and disposability over longevity and sustainability. Straw's analysis highlights how the cultural forces shaping obsolescence contribute to a waste economy that is deeply entangled with the values and practices of modern consumerism.

While many academics have analyzed the waste generated by the relentless evolution of media technologies, the growing accumulation of space junk has failed to receive the attention it deserves. Along with serious aesthetic or symbolic concerns, such as the problem of satellite trails "contaminating" images of the night sky, space debris creates many practical challenges that threaten the sustainability of space operations and exploration (Witze, 2018). One of the most pressing risks associated with space debris is the Kessler Syndrome, a scenario proposed by NASA scientist Donald J. Kessler in 1978 (Norton, 2021). This concept describes the potential for small collisions between pieces of debris to initiate a cascading chain reaction, generating even more debris and rendering certain orbital regions unusable. Such a scenario could severely hinder the ability of future spacecraft to safely exit Earth's orbit, compromising both scientific missions and commercial activities. The dangers posed by space junk are not hypothetical; they include significant risks to human life, particularly for astronauts aboard the International Space Station (ISS), which must frequently maneuver to avoid collisions with debris. Additionally, the economic implications are substantial: the destruction of operational satellites due to debris impacts can result in losses running into billions of dollars, affecting industries reliant on satellite services, such as telecommunications, weather forecasting, and global navigation systems (Klinkrad, 2006).

As the number of satellites in orbit continues to grow—driven by ventures like SpaceX's Starlink and other commercial satellite constellations—the threat of space debris becomes increasingly urgent. This hazard affects not only current space operations but also the viability of future endeavors, from deep space exploration to the expansion of satellite-based services. Addressing this issue demands the development and implementation of comprehensive strategies, including improved debris tracking, active debris removal technologies, and international regulatory frameworks, to mitigate and manage the escalating risks associated with space debris. These efforts are essential to ensuring the long-term sustainability of human activity in space.

While scientists are indispensable in highlighting the technical risks posed by space debris—such as collisions, operational hazards, and the cascading effects of the Kessler Syndrome—art and aesthetics offer a complementary lens through which we can understand the broader cultural and existential losses associated with not addressing obsolescence. By engaging with the symbolic and emotional dimensions of technological waste, art can reveal the ways in which our treatment of obsolescence shapes our relationship with progress and sustainability, especially the moral implications of filling the cosmos with relics of human activity. For instance, by emphasizing the unpleasant fact that his artworks will outlive human civilization, Paglen evokes the meaning of deep time, drawing attention to the enduring presence of space debris as a legacy of human technological ambition. Works, like *Orbital Reflector* and *The Last Pictures*, not only reveal what it means to leave behind artifacts of fleeting utility that will persist long after their functional relevance has faded but also the intangible losses that can occur when obsolescence is overlooked. As it has become clear, the proliferation of satellites and debris has fundamentally altered our experience of the night sky, obscuring its ancestral and cultural significance as a source of wonder and connection. Art can make these changes visible, creating space for reflection on how our technological pursuits impact not only practical realities but also the symbolic and emotional landscapes that define human experience.

Conclusion

In this chapter, I examined two contrasting aesthetic approaches to satellite technology, each reflecting differing political perspectives on the perception of satellites as pollution. For many in the amateur and professional astronomical communities, satellites are seen as significant visual pollutants that disrupt the pristine beauty of the night sky. They are regarded as intrusions because they represent modern technological advancements that detract from a romanticized and idyllic vision of the cosmos. Paradoxically, addressing this dilemma often requires deploying even more advanced technologies, such as artificial intelligence, to erase traces of modernity from astronomical imagery. While this technological remediation is essential for preserving scientific data, I argue that, from an aesthetic standpoint, this practice perpetuates a neoliberal governance model. By adopting an "out of sight, out of mind" mode of Anthropocene visuality, the digital erasure of satellites obscures the underlying power dynamics shaping the colonization of outer space and diminishes public awareness of the inequities embedded in space exploration and governance.

In contrast, Trevor Paglen's work adopts a radically different aesthetic approach, one that seeks to reveal rather than conceal the invisible networks orbiting above us. For Paglen, satellites are indispensable elements of the contemporary night sky, and their erasure amounts to a denial of the material realities of a new space age—one theoretically envisioned as a shared resource but, in practice, controlled by a select few. Projects, such as *The Last Pictures* and *Orbital Reflector*, exemplify this critique by foregrounding how the future of the night sky is shaped primarily by a narrow spectrum of institutional powers, dominated by military and communications industries. These entities exert immense control over space governance, often excluding broader public interests or concerns.

Paglen's work also highlights the troubling lack of communal input into critical questions surrounding the future of space. Decisions about whether humans will retain the ability to gaze upon a clear, star-filled sky, or whether low Earth orbit will remain navigable amidst an ever-growing clutter of debris, are not subject to public debate or democratic decision-making. Instead, these issues are determined by a small group of individuals and institutions whose visions for outer space rarely align with the desires or needs of the broader global community. By illuminating the forces that shape our relationship with the cosmos, Paglen advocates for a more inclusive and equitable conversation about the governance of space and the technologies that influence our perception of it, reminding us that the decisions made today will shape humanity's legacy among the stars.

Chapter Four

TEAMLAB AND THE INTERACTIVE ESTHETICS OF ARTIFICIAL DARKNESS

Introduction

For over 100,000 years, humans have formed deep spiritual and scientific connections with the cosmos, especially by observing the Milky Way—a practice now endangered by the rise of light pollution. Even a century ago, residents of modern cities like Paris could marvel at the night sky; however, today, most urban dwellers live under skies so bright that they will never witness the Milky Way, the loss of a significant cultural and ecological inheritance: not only does the diminishing visibility of the stars erase a vital source of human creativity and storytelling but it also exacerbates ecological harm, such as disrupting plant and animal reproductive cycles.

Unlike many contemporary environmental challenges that demand extensive technological, economic, and cultural transformations, light pollution is a comparatively solvable issue. Small technological adjustments, such as implementing shielded fixtures or adopting more efficient lighting systems, could significantly reduce artificial light pollution. Yet, despite these straightforward solutions, efforts to mitigate light pollution have struggled to gain widespread public support, and the natural darkness of the night sky continues to fade (Ashworth, 2023). In response, many Dark Sky initiatives have emerged, which seek to revive appreciation for the starry night and highlight its cultural, ecological, and scientific value. One prominent approach involves stargazing in protected national parks, where visitors can still experience relatively unspoiled night skies. These astro-tourist experiences provide rare opportunities for urban populations to get out of the city and reconnect with the awe and wonder of the cosmos. In chapter two, I explore how these new forms of eco-tourism frame the starry night as a pristine and timeless spectacle, evoking nostalgia for humanity's pre-industrial past. While these efforts succeed in raising awareness about the beauty of the cosmos, I argue that this romanticized approach risks oversimplifying the issue. Emphasizing purity and aesthetic wonder, while emotionally powerful, may not effectively motivate urban populations to adopt sustainable lighting practices.

In this chapter, I explore how a more familiar urban experience—visiting interactive digital art installations—can inspire a deeper appreciation for urban darkness. Traditionally, the Dark Sky movement has emphasized the value of natural or rural darkness, leveraging positive encounters with the unspoiled night sky to encourage people to rethink their relationship with darkness. However, there has been limited exploration of how artificial darkness might achieve similar outcomes. Focusing on the work of the Tokyo-based art collective, teamLab, I demonstrate how interactive digital art can transform urban spaces into immersive environments that celebrate the beauty of darkness. By combining artificial darkness with dynamic digital light shows, teamLab's installations create sensory-rich experiences that highlight the interplay between light and shadow, offering a fresh perspective on the aesthetic and emotional qualities of darkness. Additionally, these installations leverage interactive digital tools to foster social intimacy and collective engagement. By allowing visitors to influence or co-create elements of art, teamLab's work promotes a sense of connection and shared experience within urban settings. These qualities suggest that urban environments can play an important role in cultivating appreciation for darkness, presenting new opportunities to blend art, technology, and community in ways that complement the goals of the Dark Sky movement.

Artificial Darkness and Interactive Art

In recent years, scholars in the humanities have sought to challenge the deep-seated Western tradition of associating darkness with negation, chaos, irrationality, and monstrosity. Historically, darkness has been imbued with negative connotations, from moralizing narratives about "dark slums" to supernatural tales of nocturnal hauntings. In response, many scholars have emphasized the positive dimensions of darkness, highlighting its ability to evoke sensory-rich experiences of wonder and awe or to foster shared social intimacy. Activities such as stargazing in Dark Sky parks—certified areas free from light pollution—illustrate this reappraisal, as they reconnect participants with the sublime beauty of the cosmos.

While this re-evaluation of darkness spans diverse experiences, it often centers on natural darkness, understood as the absence of artificial light and closely tied to the celestial cycle of day and night. However, this focus tends to overlook the modern creation of artificial darkness, a phenomenon shaped by the rise of image-based media technologies. Artificial darkness—forms of darkness created intentionally through techniques like dimming, shadowing, and enclosure—has played a significant role in shaping modern visual culture, offering immersive, controlled environments that enable unique aesthetic and sensory experiences. As a form of darkness that is not dependent on natural astronomical rhythms, artificial darkness presents an alternative framework for understanding the aesthetics and social intimacy of gloom, showing that the value of darkness resides not solely in its natural origins but also in the capacity for artificiality to inspire creativity and appreciation in contemporary urban contexts.

In *Artificial Darkness: An Obscure History of Modern Art and Media*, Noam M. Elcott (2016) explores the pivotal role of artificial darkness in shaping modern visual culture. Elcott examines how controlled, technologically mediated darkness has been intentionally employed across various artistic practices, tracing its evolution and its influence on modernist movements such as cinema, photography, and installation art. Elcott defines "artificial darkness" as the deliberate use of darkness as an aesthetic and technological tool, transforming it from a perceived absence of light into an active agent of artistic expression. Challenging the traditional view of darkness as a negative space or passive backdrop, Elcott demonstrates how darkness has been instrumental in the development of modern art and media, revealing its capacity to direct attention, create immersive experiences, and alter perceptions, offering artists new ways to transform visual environments.

One of the most influential art movements to design with darkness was the Light and Space movement, a Los Angeles-based collective active during the 1960s and 1970s that revolutionized immersive installations by seamlessly blending light and darkness to create sublime sensory experiences. Among its many prominent figures, including Douglas Wheeler, Maria Norman, and Larry Bell, James Turrell emerged as the movement's "master of light." Renowned for his mesmerizing "walls" of light, Turrell consistently challenged viewers to reconsider their perceptual relationships with light, shadow, and darkness. Turrell's most iconic project, *Roden Crater*, exemplifies his ability to transform light and darkness into profound artistic and experiential mediums (Figure 11). Situated within an extinct volcanic crater in the Arizona desert, this ambitious, ongoing installation is designed as a monumental observatory that bridges art, astronomy, and spirituality. Featuring domes, chambers, and staircases, Roden Crater invites visitors to engage directly with celestial phenomena through carefully constructed spaces that frame the interplay of light and shadow. At the heart of the experience is a remarkable transition: visitors ascend a central staircase from a series of darkened rooms into a circular chamber of darkness, which gradually opens to reveal the infinite expanse of the night sky. This meticulously designed sequence has often been described as a spiritual or transformative journey, evoking a heightened awareness of the cosmos and the human capacity for perception. By using darkness as a canvas for light, Turrell's *Roden Crater* underscores the interplay

Figure 11. Image of Roden Crater (source: https://www.azcentral.com).

between natural light, human vision, and artificial darkness, offering a powerful exploration of how light and darkness shape our understanding of the universe.

teamLab: Digital Art and Interacting with Darkness

In the contemporary art world, the Japanese collective teamLab has emerged as a pioneering force, expanding on the sensory-rich traditions of the Light and Space movement while redefining the boundaries of interactive and participatory art. Founded in 2001, teamLab is known for its innovative use of digital technology to create immersive environments that engage visitors in multisensory, dynamic experiences. By integrating large-scale projections, mirrors, and responsive digital displays, teamLab's installations blur the lines between digital and physical worlds and foster a sense of connection between humans and the natural environment. One of teamLab's most celebrated projects is Borderless, an immersive digital art museum in Tokyo. In this groundbreaking space, artworks transcend the constraints of static frames, moving seamlessly across rooms and interacting with visitors in real time. The installations encourage exploration, creating a fluid, otherworldly environment where participants can lose themselves in a perpetual dialog between art and space. The museum exemplifies teamLab's commitment to dissolving traditional boundaries—not only between art and observer but also between art forms themselves. Another standout installation is *The Infinite Crystal Universe*, a room illuminated by thousands of suspended LED lights that respond to visitors' movements. This immersive work evokes the sensation of being surrounded by a boundless, dynamic cosmos, where the interplay of light and interaction creates a deeply personal and communal experience. Visitors are invited to engage with the installation, shaping its luminous patterns and fostering a sense of co-creation.

While teamLab's work has been widely praised for its innovative use of technology and its immersive, participatory nature, little attention has been given to the role artificial darkness plays in these experiences. For instance, in their *Microcosmoses* installation, visitors step into a darkened room containing an interactive rail system with moving orbs that light up and change color (Figure 12). As people approach the orbs, the lights shift in color and speed,

Figure 12. Microcosmoses (source: https://www.teamlab.art/w/microcosmoses/#modal-3).

transmitting these changes to the nearest orbs, creating a cascading effect. The experience of navigating the installation evokes a peculiar sensation of displacement and disorientation due to the room's scale. The circulating orbs resemble a cosmos of orbiting stars, making the visitor's body feel immense, as if one were traversing the Milky Way. Similarly, in *The Infinite Crystal Universe*, visitors wander through a darkened space filled with strings of LED lights that change color and flash in various patterns. At times, the room evokes a sense of intergalactic travel, while at other moments, the pulsating lights resemble shooting stars. Like *Microcosmoses*, this installation is also interactive—visitors can use their smartphones to create patterns of light that are projected into the "universe" and influence the entire room. In these installations, teamLab masterfully uses artificial darkness to evoke the awe and wonder of traditional stargazing, reimagining cosmic experiences within a gallery setting. Through immersive darkness and dynamic illuminated elements, they replicate the sensation of observing celestial phenomena, fostering a profound connection between visitors and the cosmos.

Perhaps the most creative and interactive installation that allows visitors to experience the phenomenological changes involved in the movement from night to day is *Four Seasons, a 1000 Years, Terraced Rice Field* (Figure 13). In this exhibition, teamLab uses real-time digital information and projection mappings to simulate the natural transitions of light and darkness. This installation draws upon live weather data to depict the evolving ecosystem of an ancient Japanese rice field. As the digital landscape mirrors the natural

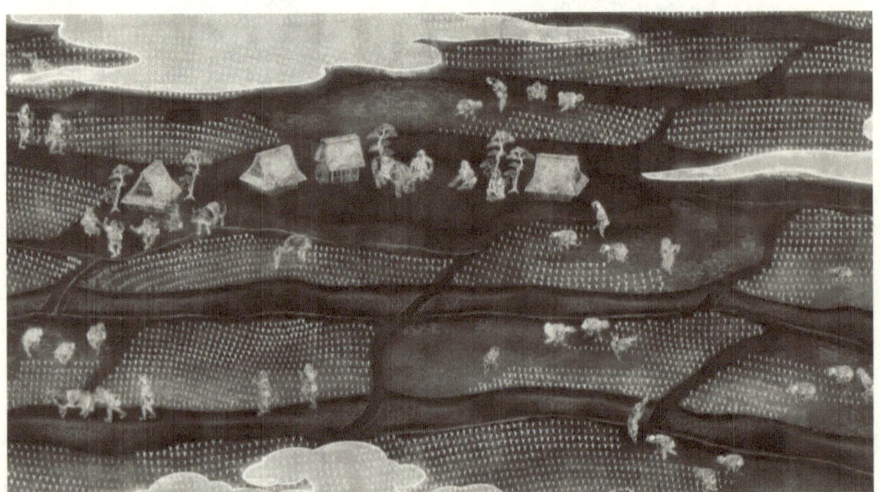

Figure 13. *Four Seasons, a 1000 Years, Terraced Rice Field* (source: https://www.teamlab.art/w/tashibunosho/#modal-8).

progression of time, it transitions seamlessly from day to night: the brightness of dawn gives way to the gradual dimming of evening, immersing viewers in an ever-changing interplay of light and shadow. By aligning the digital display with real-world temporal and ecological rhythms, the work offers a continuously evolving experience that reflects the passage of time and the interconnectedness of light and darkness in the natural world. The effect is both mesmerizing and educational, allowing visitors to engage with nature's cycles within an artificial environment.

In addition to creating mesmerizing gallery experiences with artificial darkness, teamLab has also extended its innovative installations to urban parks and historical sites, transforming natural darkness into a dynamic canvas for digital art. By blending LED lights, projection mapping, and interactive displays, these nighttime installations foster new connections between art, technology, and the environment, immersing visitors in a reimagined relationship with the natural world. For example, at Nagai Botanical Garden in Osaka, teamLab draws attention to the garden's beauty by animating its landscapes after dark. Using digital techniques, the installation fuses light and sound with nature, creating a sensory-rich experience. One of the installation's signature features involves a series of oval orbs that glow and shift colors in response to visitors' movements. As people explore, motion sensors trigger visual and auditory changes, turning the pathways, trees, and flowers into vibrant, living artworks. This interplay between light, darkness, and motion not only reinvigorates the park's landscape but also deepens visitors' appreciation for the coexistence of technology and nature. Similarly, teamLab's installation at Toji Temple in Kyoto offers a striking blend of historical architecture and digital art. The ancient temple grounds are illuminated with LED lights and images of interactive digital flowers are projected on the five-storied pagoda. Particularly captivating is the floating resonating lamps in the Hyotan Pond, where illuminated glass lamps ripple with changing colors and sounds, creating a tranquil, dreamlike ambiance.

In these and many other installations, teamLab transforms the traditional art gallery experience by using artificial light and darkness to create interactive, awe-inspiring digital environments that evoke the sense of wonder typically associated with the "pristine" night. In conventional art museums, visitors are accustomed to navigating well-lit, divided rooms where individual artworks are displayed separately, encouraging isolated and contemplative viewing. In contrast, teamLab's installations invite visitors to become active participants in the art-making process, as their movements and behaviors are captured as live data that directly influences the unfolding of the artworks. This dynamic and responsive interaction blurs the line between the viewer and the art, establishing a seamless connection with the digital imagery.

teamLab refers to this immersive experience as "ultrasubjective space," a mode of representation that integrates digital technology with spatial perspectives found in premodern Japanese art (Lee, 2022). By incorporating visitors' actions into the creation of unique atmospheres featuring different forms of darkness, teamLab's artworks not only make participants more attuned to how ecological systems are continually shaped and reshaped by human activity but also emphasize that artificial darkness is far from a neutral backdrop. Instead, it plays a vital role in the sensory nature of art installations. Like experiences with natural darkness, teamLab's creation of artificial darkness can evoke feelings of awe by transforming sensory perceptions and crafting environments that contrast sharply with the light-filled surroundings of everyday life. These experiences align with Tim Edensor's exploration of how darkness can "re-enchant" our encounters with the world, leading to moments of awe by transforming familiar spaces into realms of depth and intrigue. By using artificial darkness to evoke such feelings, teamLab reimagines how darkness can be a source of enchantment, inviting viewers to perceive and interact with space in profound, multisensory ways.

In *Shivers Down Your Spine: Cinema, Museums, and the Immersive View*, Alison Griffiths (2008) challenges the conventional understanding of museum experiences as primarily intellectual and observational. Drawing parallels to cinema's use of space, sound, and visuals to captivate audiences, Griffiths argues that interactive museums similarly move beyond passive observation. By blending education with entertainment, these spaces offer multisensory experiences that engage visitors physically and emotionally. "Immersion," Griffiths explains, "is the sensation of entering a space that distinguishes itself as somehow separate from the world, rejecting traditional spectatorship for a more bodily involvement, allowing the viewer freedom to navigate the space." Griffiths' understanding of interactivity underscores how immersive experiences invite visitors to actively participate and inhabit the exhibit, transforming them from passive observers into engaged participants. Through this integration of sensory stimulation, spatial design, and emotional resonance, immersive museum environments mirror cinematic techniques, offering visitors a dynamic and embodied connection to the narratives on display.

While there are many ways museums use aesthetics to evoke immersion, teamLab harnesses the affective powers of artificial darkness to heighten emotional involvement with their works. Across their oeuvre, the interactive play between spectators, light, and darkness creates otherworldly experiences that dissolve the traditional distance between viewer and artwork. In doing so, teamLab challenges the notion of authenticity often tied to maintaining critical distance from works of art. Walter Benjamin (2008), in his influential essay "The Work of Art in the Age of Mechanical Reproduction," argues that an artwork's aura—its sense of authenticity and authority—stems from its unique existence in time and space. This aura is reinforced by the physical experience of encountering the artwork in person, as well as its history and provenance. Importantly, Benjamin emphasizes that aura relies on the viewer's spatial and emotional distance from the work, fostering a contemplative, almost reverent mode of engagement.

By contrast, teamLab's installations collapse this distance, rejecting the static, observational model of art viewing in favor of active participation. Darkness plays a critical role in this process: it immerses viewers in sensory environments where their presence, motion, and touch trigger dynamic transformations. This heightened intimacy between the viewer and the work undermines the traditional aura described by Benjamin, as teamLab replaces contemplative distance with embodied immediacy. Instead of encountering the artwork as a fixed object of historical or cultural significance, spectators become part of a fluid, ever-changing environment that prioritizes emotional connection and interaction over static authenticity. In this way, teamLab reimagines the viewer's relationship with art, offering a participatory experience where darkness becomes the medium for dissolving boundaries between subject and object.

This use of darkness to create multisensory experiences of closeness and proximity aligns with a growing body of scholarship emphasizing the importance of the senses in fostering meaningful connections with art. For example, Guo et al., writing about the role of multi-sensory engagement in enhancing touristic experiences, state: "Multisensory cues can provide a personalized, co-creative, and involving experience to tourists, and enhance the memorability of the experience. The richer the multisensory experiences are, the longer tourists' memory of such experiences lasts, which in turn triggers their positive emotional, attitudinal, and behavioral intentions toward the visit destination."

Similarly, Kim Knight (2015) argues that "authenticity is augmented by closeness," suggesting that tactile, interactive encounters with artwork allow viewers to form personal, embodied connections that create a new kind of aura. Rather than relying on the viewer's distance to establish the artwork's authority—as Walter Benjamin theorized—Knight reframes authenticity as something that emerges through proximity and active participation. This idea of intimacy resonates with the works of the philosopher, Karen Barad, who argues that touch goes beyond creating a connection; it also has profound ethical implications. Barad (2012) writes: "Touching is a matter of response. Each of 'us' is constituted in response-ability. Each of 'us' is constituted as responsible for the other, as the other" (215). Here, touch operates as an affective mode of communication, creating a physical and sensuous bridge between the human body and the artwork. Touch becomes relational, not merely facilitating contact but also evoking response-ability—a shared responsibility for the engagement.

Though darkness has long been associated with danger and death, in the works of teamLab artificial darkness amplifies the affective and relational power of touch. With reduced visual cues, the human body compensates by heightening its reliance on touch, intensifying sensitivity to tactile sensations. As Barad's theory suggests, this heightened state of touch deepens our relationship with the environment, fostering a more embodied, ethical interaction with the digital artwork. In dark or dimly lit settings, touch becomes integral to spatial navigation—extending hands to explore, detect obstacles, or orient ourselves—demonstrating how darkness transforms sensory perception. This enhanced reliance on touch within teamLab's interactive, darkened installations not only deepens immersion but also evokes a physical and emotional intimacy that bridges the gap between viewer, artwork, and space.

Re-enchanting the City: Artificial Darkness, Light Festivals, and Social Solidarity

Traditionally, the urban night has been associated with an assortment of social problems, dangers, and risks. From the perils of increased criminality to the lonely solitude of reduced social activity, the urban night has long been treated as a time requiring increased vigilance and surveillance. As Murray Melbin (1987) has argued, the perception that night is a temporal frontier that must be colonized through technological and cultural developments, such as street lighting and extended working hours, has meant that urban forms of nocturnal sociability have not always been accepted by mainstream society.

To change this perception of the night, new forms of nighttime tourism have emerged, which attempt to move the urban night beyond traditional night-time economies based on drinking. One of the most well-known ways in which the night has been reclaimed as a time for communal activity, creativity, and shared celebration is through light festivals. Indeed, in cities across the world, urban light festivals have emerged as significant cultural events, transforming public spaces through the creative interplay of light, art, and darkness. Often taking place in public parks, plazas, and streets at night, light festivals have not only been used to revitalize the economic life of cities, but they reclaim urban spaces as sites of collective experience, shared wonder, and community-building. By making public spaces more inviting and visually stimulating, light festivals encourage people to linger and interact, breaking down the social fragmentation often caused by urban design and spatial inequalities. Beyond their aesthetic appeal, light festivities can foster social intimacy and solidarity by encouraging interactions among diverse groups of people and reshaping the way cities are perceived and experienced (Alves, 2007; Edesnosr, 2014; Sumartojo, 2015).

Since light festivals invite people to gather in urban spaces after dark, they can break down barriers of solitude and transform the nocturnal city into an illuminated stage for collective experience. Enlivening the night with interactive light installations, urban light festivals allow cities to redefine nighttime as a time of connection and creativity rather than the urban malaise and alienation sometimes associated with urban places. As Giordano and Ong (2017) write,

> Illuminating sites, thus, can work towards a greater sense of navigation for visitors at night and a greater appreciation of the thematic elements of the city and its elements—highlighted and facilitated via the spectacle of calculated illumination. As acts and practices geared towards theming urban places and simulating fantasy-scapes, light festivals and their enchanting lighting schemes are appreciated and consumed for the ways in which they add to the experience of cities and urban areas. (712)

While these festivals may not always create authentic experiences of local places, this reclamation of the night marks a cultural shift where the spectacle of the illuminated city can generate vibrant and enchanting spaces. Urban tourists, who may otherwise retreat to private spaces after dark, are drawn into public areas to interact with one another, fostering a renewed sense of community.

According to Tim Edensor, the transformative appeal of urban light festivals involves the ways they redesign the atmosphere of the city, creating conditions conducive to social intimacy. Edensor (2015b) argues that light installations can produce "affective atmospheres" that influence emotional and sensory responses, encouraging people to engage more closely with their surroundings and with one another. Light festivals often use artistic lighting to transform familiar urban environments into enchanting, otherworldly spaces. By replacing harsh, functional lighting with softer, dynamic, and colorful illuminations, these festivals create a sense of wonder that draws people together. For instance, interactive light installations that respond to touch, sound, or movement encourage playfulness and shared exploration, breaking down social barriers and enabling spontaneous interactions between strangers. In this way, light festivals generate spaces of social intimacy, where participants feel connected not only to the art but also to each other. People navigating through illuminated installations often share glances, gestures, and conversations, fostering a sense of closeness and camaraderie. These shared experiences, shaped by the affective power of light, bring urban residents together in ways that transcend the anonymity and isolation often associated with city life.

Similarly, darkness, often seen as a barrier to social connection, has been reimagined in recent years to create novel cultural and touristic experiences that foster social intimacy. Events such as dining in the dark, concerts in the dark, and black-out theatrical performances, challenge conventional associations of darkness with fear and isolation, transforming gloom into a medium for heightened sensory awareness and shared vulnerability. Dining in the dark, for example, invites participants to enjoy meals in pitch-black settings, eliminating visual distractions and encouraging people to focus on the taste, smell, sound, and touch of the cuisine. Sharing a meal in complete darkness can also break down social barriers, as participants engage in conversation without preconceptions based on appearance, encouraging openness and trust. Similarly, all-dark concerts use darkness to create immersive musical experiences that prioritize listening and emotional connection. By removing visual stimuli, these concerts allow audiences to focus entirely on the auditory experience, creating an intimate bond between performers and listeners. Here, darkness amplifies the emotional impact of music, as participants feel more attuned to subtle shifts in sound and rhythm. Finally, immersive theater productions, such as Sleep No More and other site-specific performances, have also explored the use of darkness to create interactive and intimate experiences. In these performances, participants navigate dimly lit or dark spaces, often interacting directly with actors and the environment. Darkness heightens the sense of mystery and exploration, encouraging audiences to rely on touch, sound, and intuition as they move through the performance. This multisensory engagement fosters a sense of shared adventure and connection, as participants navigate the unknown together. In each of these examples, artificial light and darkness are used not as barriers but as a medium for sensory enrichment and social connection. By removing visual distractions or heightening the visual senses, these experiences foster intimacy, vulnerability, and trust among participants. Artificial light and darkness, therefore, become a tool for creating memorable, immersive cultural and touristic experiences that emphasize human connection and shared presence.

As highly participatory works that require the involvement of visitors, many of teamLab's exhibitions use artificial darkness as a medium for creating social intimacy and solidarity. Within these carefully curated darkened spaces, individuals are encouraged to not only engage with the art but also with one another in ways that challenge conventional viewing experiences, fostering deeper connections and shared wonder. As mentioned previously, unlike conventional galleries where lighting often isolates artworks and reinforces individual contemplation, teamLab's darkened spaces create an egalitarian environment where the focus is on collective participation in the artwork. As many scholars like Tim Edensor have shown, in darkness, the viewer's identity can sink into the backdrop, as their body becomes a silhouette or indistinct shadowy presence among other silhouettes in the museum. This invisibility can help reduce the self-consciousness of the participant and encourage a sense of anonymity. In darkness people often revert to a nocturnal self, where anonymity creates a space for vulnerability and openness, enabling individuals to engage more freely with one another. Viewers become participants rather than passive spectators, exploring and interacting with the works in ways that foster organic social interactions. Thus, by allowing participants to feel secure and uninhibited in the art gallery setting, teamLab's use of darkness breaks down many of the social barriers of art institutions, democratizing the art experience by making it accessible to all. The removal of hierarchies is particularly significant in fostering solidarity. In the darkened environments of teamLab's installations, differences in age, gender, social status, and background fade into obscurity. Visitors can theoretically experience the art as equals, unified by their engagement with the shared space. This sense of equality allows for spontaneous, collaborative interactions that might not occur in more brightly lit, structured gallery settings.

For instance, in teamLab's Borderless exhibition, installations such as *Forest of Resonating Lamps* invite visitors into immersive, low-light environments, where the interplay of light and reflections creates an ethereal and dreamlike atmosphere. Visitors move carefully through the space, aware of the presence of others yet often unable to distinguish faces. This shared experience of wonder fosters quiet, unspoken connections between viewers, who share the intimacy of the moment without the need for verbal communication. Similarly, in *Universe of Water Particles*, cascading waterfalls of light react to the movements of viewers. In these spaces, children and adults alike explore the digital waterfalls together, with no distinction in status or role. The darkness removes the visual markers that might otherwise separate individuals, encouraging collective play and participation. Finally, in *Sketch Aquarium*, visitors draw fish on paper, which are then digitally transformed and projected into a virtual aquatic environment. As the space darkens, the vibrant, illuminated fish come to life, swimming alongside other participants' creations. In this collaborative environment, individuals become co-creators of the artwork, fostering a sense of shared accomplishment and connection. Darkness adds to the magic of the moment, emphasizing the collective creativity at play.

As mentioned earlier, a common response to teamLab's works involves the way they use darkness to amplify the emotional impact of their artworks. Darkness heightens the vibrancy of light and color, creating moments of visual and emotional spectacle. The stark contrast between darkness and light evokes feelings of wonder, awe, and even transcendence, which are often more profound when experienced collectively. In works like *Floating Flower Garden* or *Planets*, visitors step into environments where darkness allows illuminated elements to appear as though suspended in mid-air. These surreal spaces blur the lines between reality and imagination, fostering a sense of childlike curiosity and wonder. Importantly, these feelings are not experienced in isolation. The presence of others enhances the sense of shared awe, transforming individual reactions into collective experiences. Psychologically, moments of awe have been shown to strengthen social bonds and promote prosocial behaviors. When people experience wonder together, they are more likely to feel connected and empathetic toward one another. teamLab's exhibitions capitalize on this phenomenon by creating environments that elicit awe through their scale, beauty, and interactivity. Darkness intensifies these feelings by heightening the contrast and mystery of the artwork, inviting viewers to share in the experience of discovery and marvel.

One of the common critiques of teamLab is that their works are tourist traps, where endless tourists line up to take selfies for their social media feeds. While it is true that teamLab's exhibitions accommodate large numbers of visitors, their strategic use of darkness still offers pockets of intimacy within the broader tourist experience. While many of their installations are quite bold and dramatic, and take on a larger-than-life sensibility, other installations use darkness to foster moments of quiet reflection and connection even within the museum's crowded spaces. In their work, *Flowers and People Cannot be Controlled but Live Together*, for example, visitors walk through a series of darkened rooms that feature flowers that bud, blossom, and die according to different seasonal changes. The installation is not prerecorded, but uses a computer program that converts the movements and actions of the visitors into signals that alter the flowers. As multiple people move throughout the rooms, the artwork unfolds in an unpredictable manner, as the interaction of small pockets of people causes the flowers to change color and create different tonalities of light. The result is a symphony of dynamic change and vitality, which provides the visitor with a shared sense of commonality and accomplishment.

Similarly, in *Flowers Bloom in an Infinite Universe inside a Teacup*, visitors participate in what appears to be a traditional Japanese tea ceremony. However, by using projection mapping and digital technologies which respond to the individual actions of each participant, the installation creates a novel and wonderous feeling of infinite change. As long as one of the participants has tea in their cup, flowers will bloom inside; likewise, picking up a teacup causes the flowers to scatter throughout the room. Like with *Flowers and People*, since the installation responds to the interactions of all the people participating in the tea ceremony, the room offers visitors a chance to gain insight not only into the ephemeral nature of life but also how this experience is shared and modified by all others in the ceremony.

Conclusion

In this chapter, I have outlined some ways art-based experiences with artificial darkness align with recent initiatives to preserve darkness. Traditionally, dark sky advocates have turned toward the wondrous sensory experiences and social intimacy of natural darkness to encourage people to recognize the cultural and aesthetic beauty of the night. I argue that alongside these positive reappraisals of natural darkness are similar phenomenological experiences created by artificial darkness. Through their interactive art installations, which use real-time data from participants to modulate a wide variety of digital ecologies, teamLab not only produces captivating experiences that attune people to the wonders of the dark but also enhances social intimacy among visitors. While many argue that natural darkness offers a more authentic encounter with the unspoiled night sky, this chapter shows how meaningful experiences with artificial darkness can maintain many conservationist advantages. For example, as the earth's population becomes ever more urban, experiences with artificial darkness can become more accessible and popular. Since art installations are often located in urban or suburban areas where people live, more people may have the opportunity to visit these touristic locations than pristine nature parks, which are becoming increasingly remote and require extensive travel. Likewise, artificial darkness experiences can be replicated in multiple locations, reaching a wider audience than any single natural Dark Sky site. This scalability ensures that the message about preserving darkness can spread to more people. Artificial darkness may even be more inclusive. Not everyone feels comfortable in natural dark settings, as they can evoke fear or disorientation. Artificial environments can simulate darkness in a way that feels safe and welcoming, broadening their appeal to a diverse audience, including children and individuals with disabilities.

These are just a few of the advantages artificial darkness brings to the effort to preserve darkness. Yet, despite the potential advantages of urban art installations, there have been very few attempts, among either artists or dark-sky proponents, to convert these wondrous, intimate experiences with artificial darkness into educational messages about the value of darkness or the losses that come from light pollution. For example, while teamLab frames its art installations as a form of ecological awareness, to my knowledge they have never made any attempts to link their curated forms of artificial darkness to the growing ecological challenges of urban light pollution. This, I believe, is a missed opportunity. The popularity of teamLab is a testament to the joyous communal experiences their art continues to provide. So much of this creative power resides in the shared beauty of artificial darkness, which not only offers artists and audiences alike a canvas for exploration, creativity, and contemplation but also ways of appreciating sensory-rich experiences that do not fall into the rhetorical traps of the pure and pristine.

Chapter Five

DECOLONIZING THE ARCTIC NIGHT

Introduction

The violent seizure of Indigenous lands and centuries of forced migration are well-known traumas of Western colonialism. However, a lesser-known colonial threat that has taken shape recently involves the aggressive pursuit of outer space by affluent corporations, which jeopardizes Indigenous Peoples' ancestral ties to the night sky. By 2030, it is projected that over 10,000 small satellites will occupy low Earth orbit as the satellite industry works to expand broadband internet access, particularly in remote and rural areas (Brodie, 2020). While this technological development could provide tangible benefits to many Indigenous communities by offering reliable internet services that support education, healthcare, and economic opportunities, it also carries profound cultural and environmental costs. The proliferation of satellite constellations, for example, contributes significantly to light pollution, diminishing the visibility of the stars. Referred to as astro-colonization, this phenomenon poses a threat to Indigenous stargazing traditions, which are deeply intertwined with cultural identity, navigation, storytelling, and spiritual practices (Ferreira, 2021).

This threat to Indigenous astronomical knowledge is doubly troubling. First, Western science has historically overlooked the valuable empirical contributions made by Indigenous astronomers, whose knowledge systems often reflect generations of careful observation and interaction with the natural world (Hamacher, 2023). Indigenous cosmologies have informed practical applications, such as navigation and seasonal planning, while also offering profound insights into the relational dynamics between Earth and the cosmos. The continued marginalization of Indigenous knowledge systems thus represents a significant loss for humanity's collective understanding of the universe. Second, the absence of robust international regulations governing the current "rush to space" exacerbates this threat. Without oversight, the uncontrolled proliferation of satellite technologies risks severing Indigenous Peoples' connections to the ancient stories, practices, and cultural identities intricately tied to the constellations. As Venkatesan et al. (2020)

argue, "Treating space as the 'Wild West' frontier that requires conquering continues to incentivize claims by those who are well-resourced. It will also bring all the wounding and long-term consequences that imperial colonizing policies brought on Earth—now poised to be magnified on a cosmic scale for the most vulnerable marginalized communities on Earth, including Indigenous peoples" (1046).

Astro-colonization can thus be understood as an extension of the colonial processes that have historically dispossessed Indigenous Peoples of their lands, waters, and skies. By altering the celestial landscapes that have guided their cosmologies for millennia, the satellite industry risks perpetuating a new form of cultural erasure. For many Indigenous cultures, the stars are not merely distant lights but active participants in a shared history, embodying ancestors, knowledge systems, and sacred teachings. The disruption of these connections amounts to a form of cultural genocide, as it undermines the intergenerational transmission of knowledge and traditions tied to the night sky.

Decolonizing the Night

Although the current conquest of outer space features a series of new "billionaire actors" who are privatizing low Earth orbit with minimal public accountability, the detrimental effects of framing space as a frontier are not unprecedented. In her examination of Martin Heidegger's philosophy of technology, Mary-Jane Rubenstein (2008) notes that when humans treat the planet as a technological resource, they not only presume themselves to be "lords of the earth" but also engage in a violent mindset that reduces everything to mere calculation. She writes, "Trying to master the cosmos by making of it a technological stockpile, 'man' ends up becoming part of the stockpile." Furthermore, according to the philosopher Byung-Chul Han (2017), Heidegger's key insight is that, in our fast-paced modern age, the rapid advancement of technology not only exploits space for capitalist gain but also disrupts the tranquility of time. In our time of swift capitalist accumulation, time itself becomes fragmented, losing its connection to the natural cycles of cosmic duration. Heidegger characterizes this drive for speed as an inability to "bear the stillness of hidden growth" and a "blindness to what is truly momentary, which is not fleeting but opens up eternity" (Han, 2017). As Han elaborates, for the later Heidegger, the good life arises from the "silent harmony" of the changing seasons or the eternal transition from night to day.

In this chapter, my goal is to decolonize the night by utilizing three forms of Indigenous media to highlight the cultural losses that emerge from "astro-colonization." In doing so, I aim to align my research with several distinguished decolonizing initiatives that challenge the Western tendency to link darkness and the night with the "uncivilized other." For instance, in 2021, Concordia University made history in Canada by decolonizing its physics program. The "Decolonizing Light" project investigates methods to decolonize science by revitalizing Indigenous knowledge and cultivating a culture of critical reflection on science's connection to colonialism. One of their most exciting goals is to establish Indigenous stargazing as a foundational element of contemporary astronomy. In a similar vein, geographers Tim Edensor and Nick Dunn (2021) have made noteworthy progress in reversing Western colonial perspectives on darkness, which view nighttime as an anti-Enlightenment force that stigmatizes non-Western cultures. As they express:

> From medieval times [...] darkness has symbolised 'pagan obscurantism—deviancy, monstrosity, diabolism.' It is hardly surprising that in a culture saturated with widespread beliefs that a host of powerful supernatural forces lurked in dark corners, the night held multifarious terrors for most people. The devil carried out his work at night, and sinister hobgoblins, ghouls, ghosts, witches, demons and dark elves could be discerned in shadows and murky shapes. These superstitious beliefs about the dark were fueled by Christian orthodoxies which drew on biblical passages to underline absolute distinctions between a malign darkness and a godly realm of light.

To explore how the depiction of darkness as a binary opposition between evil and divine light is tied to ongoing institutional racism, I will analyze three contemporary examples of Indigenous nocturnal media: Jennie Williams' short film *Nalujuk Night*, Tanya Tagaq's novel *Split Tooth*, and the HBO series *True Detective: Night Country*. Through an analysis of these media, I hope to challenge and dismantle three pervasive myths about Indigenous experiences with darkness. The first involves the myth of extreme social isolation during the polar night. Common media representations of the polar night often depict Indigenous communities as isolated and disconnected from the world during extended periods of darkness. By contrast, *Nalujuk Night* captures the dynamic cultural and communal activities that occur during this time, illustrating the vibrant social networks and shared traditions that thrive despite environmental extremes. The second myth involves Indigenous cultural primitivism: Western narratives have historically portrayed Indigenous Peoples as bound to a "primitive" existence, particularly when juxtaposed with the Enlightenment's valorization of light as progress and civilization. Tanya Tagaq's *Split Tooth* defies this reductive view by weaving together myth, memory, and modernity, demonstrating the sophisticated interplay between tradition and contemporary experiences within Indigenous cosmologies. And finally, I will explore the myth of Indigenous victimhood: media often reduces Indigenous narratives to stories of victimhood, erasing the agency, resilience, and creativity of Indigenous communities. The HBO series *True Detective: Night Country* provides a nuanced portrayal of Indigenous characters, emphasizing their complexity, strength, and adaptability while confronting broader themes of systemic injustice and environmental degradation. Together, these works reveal that Indigenous experiences with the night go far beyond the mass media's stereotypical portrayals. Not only do they highlight the night as a profound space for cultural expression, scientific insight, and communal resilience, but they also showcase how darkness has historically been a wellspring of creativity, adaptability, and strength for Indigenous artists and communities.

Myth One: The Harsh Polar Night

In the gallery description for "Spirits of the Night," an Inuit abstract print by Myra Kukiiyaut (1989), the Arctic night is imagined as a hostile place brimming with dangers: "The harshness and randomness of life in the Arctic," the caption declares, "ensured that the Inuit lived constantly in fear of unseen forces (Figure 14). A run of bad luck could end an entire community, and begging potentially angry and vengeful but unseen powers for the necessities of day-to-day survival is a common consequence of a precarious existence, even in modern society." Although the label explores some fascinating Inuit legends, its emphasis on the night's hostility and insecurity perpetuates one of the most persistent colonial myths about the Arctic: that living in a relentless, brutal, and alien environment where the polar night results in extreme social isolation, the fate of Inuit people hinges solely on the ominous caprices of luck.

In her analysis of Canadian literature's depiction of the Arctic, Margaret Atwood (1995) also notes that many white writers portray the North as extremely inhospitable, especially during the polar night. These portrayals often emphasize the night's otherworldliness, especially the settler's fear of transforming into one of many Indigenous cannibalistic monsters. For example, many Canadian writers have obsessed over the early settler's fascination with the Windigo, a flesh-eating spirit that preys on human greed and weakness. This creature, Atwood writes, symbolizes the harshness of Arctic life by associating the extreme mental anguish caused by the polar night with scarcity and selfishness. What Atwood doesn't mention, unfortunately, is that the idea that Arctic darkness induces severe mental distress is a colonial construct, originating from the so-called "arctic sickness" or "piblokto" identified by early European settlers. Arctic sickness is a condition believed to be linked to social deprivation during the polar night. However, recent research has demonstrated that this mental disorder was not caused by the

Figure 14. "Spirits of the Night" by Myra Kukiiyaut (source: DaVic Gallery, https://nativecanadianarts.com/gallery/spirits-of-the-night/).

Arctic's long and isolating darkness but was instead a symptom of the violence inflicted upon Indigenous Peoples by colonization (Lyle, 1995).

If, as Atwood suggests, stories featuring ghouls, monsters, and mental disorders mirror a society's distorted fears of the Other, then what these settler anxieties regarding the Arctic night reveal is a widespread misconception about Indigenous Peoples' actual experiences with darkness. Contrary to being a barren and harsh ordeal or a place of bleak desolation challenging one's mental resilience, the night for many Indigenous Peoples is a period rich with socialization, storytelling, wonder, and reflection. As Charlotte Damm (2016) explains, the Arctic night was not a uniform experience of isolation but rather a time marked by significant diversity:

> For the Inuinnait in the eastern Canadian Arctic [...] the 'time of the ice-sheet' was traditionally the time of community life and long evenings spent in the igloo [...] Storytelling appears to have been a popular activity on long, dark winter nights. Likewise, in some regions, the winter solstice period was also a time for extensive travel, to spend the festive period with friends and relatives elsewhere.

A recent film that disrupts colonial narratives about the harsh Arctic night is *Nalujuk Night* (2021), a black-and-white documentary by Inuk filmmaker Jennie Williams. The film examines the integral role that darkness plays in Indigenous social rituals and community life, offering a refreshing perspective that challenges stereotypes of the polar night as isolating or desolate. Set in Nunatsiavut, the homeland of Labrador's Inuit, the documentary centers on an annual winter night celebration held on old Christmas Day. During this event, locals gather in the winter darkness to await the arrival of the Nalujuit (Heathens)—ghostly figures who cross the sea ice to playfully frighten children. These eerie, otherworldly characters, with their hunched, animalistic appearances, bring a sense of suspense and exhilaration to the celebration. While the century-old tradition has been influenced by Moravian settlers and incorporates elements resembling Christian Christmas festivities, *Nalujuk Night* departs from colonial portrayals of light and darkness as symbolic binaries. Instead of focusing on the "light" of God as a central motif, the film embraces darkness as a vital element of community cohesion and cultural expression.

Through its focus on an Indigenous nocturnal celebration, *Nalujuk Night* highlights the ritualistic power of darkness. By framing darkness as the central medium for fostering social connection and preserving Inuit collective knowledge, the film envisions the night as the environmental backdrop for what James Carey (1989) describes as the ritualistic function of media. According to Carey, media are not simply vehicles for transmitting information but integral to maintaining shared beliefs and collective identity. "A ritual view of communication," Carey writes, "is directed not toward the extension of messages in space but toward the maintenance of society in time; not the act of imparting information but the representation of shared beliefs" (18). Thus, according to Carey, by engaging in various media rituals, society participates in a symbolic process through which reality is constructed, maintained, repaired, and transformed. This ritualistic understanding of the night aligns with Robert Hensey's (2016) observation that throughout history, darkness has served as a "social theatre" for rites of passage, offering the ambiguity and liminality necessary to distinguish the sacred from the profane. Whether in early Christian cave worship or French peasant rituals conducted in shadowy forests to evade social elites, darkness provides a stage for symbolic renewal (Palmer, 2000).

Originating in Greenland and integrating with the Moravian Christian missionary belief system, the tradition of Nalujuk features three ghouls of the winter night, which some interpret as representing the wise men who visited Jesus at his birth. However, unlike most Christian celebrations that celebrate the birth of Jesus with abundant light, the Nalujuk tradition brings ghoulish figures out of the shadows to instill fear in young children, who are encouraged to display bravery and face the ominous aspects of the dark

(Richling, 1980). As Jannelle Barbour comments, the evening often begins with the Nalujuit chasing children through the town: "If caught, children must sing a song to appease the Nalujuit, with 'Surotsit Katitse' being the most common. If a child is suspected of misbehavior, they are chased and given a 'light' beating" (Nalujuit: Intangible Cultural Heritage).

In *Naluk Night*, Williams offers a joyful and lighthearted interpretation of the "terrors" that lurk in the night, emphasizing how the unique atmosphere of darkness enhances the collective experience. Rather than casting the night as a void or a space of fear, *Nalujuk Night* presents it as a dynamic and creative time, integral to maintaining social bonds and cultural traditions. Through its exploration of this Inuit winter ritual, the film reframes darkness not as a force to be feared or conquered but as a space of connection, playfulness, and enduring cultural vitality. In one scene, a mother and her three young children sit quietly at home, awaiting a visit from the Nalujuit. Although the children are calm and silent,. their eyes reveal a different story, reflecting a quiet terror. Through scenes like this, the film illustrates how darkness can transform everyday domestic life into a time of wonder, where fantasy and fear serve as precarious testing grounds for feelings of fellowship and belonging. By doing so, *Nalujuk Night* challenges colonial frameworks that stigmatize the night and Arctic life as bleak or uncivilized, celebrating instead the richness and resilience of Indigenous traditions rooted in darkness.

Myth Two: Split Tooth and the Erotic Night

In the introduction, I discussed how decolonizing modern science involves recognizing Indigenous understandings of the stars as some of the earliest empirical systems of astronomical knowledge. As Māori astronomy scholar Rangi Mātāmua emphasizes, "Look at what our ancestors did to navigate here—you don't do that on myths and legends, you do that on science" (Hamacher, 2023). While decolonizing the night involves modern science's acknowledgement of Indigenous astronomy, it also entails understanding how Indigenous star stories enable communities to heal from the wounds of colonialism's violent legacies. As Annette S. Lee, a First Nations Lakota woman, astrophysicist, and professional artist, illustrates, for Indigenous communities, the stars are not just celestial objects to be observed and measured; they are living entities, deeply embedded in cultural identity, spirituality, and communal well-being. As Lee observes:

> Star knowledge brings a sense of purpose, a sense of hope, a lifeline that each person is connected to [...] to the bigger whole, the stars, the Universe. Those stars are more than just balls of gas. When we

> do Indigenous science, those stars are our oldest relatives. A sense of connectedness is a unique part of Indigenous science. In Western science, knowledge is often considered separate from the people who discover it, while Indigenous cultures see knowledge as intricately connected to people. It's not like we're just outside observers watching this. We're a part of it. (Peterschmidt 2020)

By intertwining science, culture, and art, Indigenous astronomy demonstrates that understanding the cosmos is not only about discovery but also about connection: star stories are pathways for meaning-making, fostering intergenerational learning and strengthening ties to the natural world. In this section, I explore how Tanya Tagaq's wondrous and supernatural novel *Split Tooth* presents the polar night as an erotic space-time, where star stories can help Indigenous Peoples heal from the scars of colonial violence. Using the aesthetic framework of what Cherokee scholar Daniel Heath Justice (2017) describes as "Indigenous Wonderworks," the novel uses two contrasting forms of darkness to explore a young woman's "otherworldly" journey of resilience and recovery from systemic violence and domestic abuse. On the one hand, Tagaq presents the narrator's harrowing encounters with trauma through what I term the "colonial night"—a haunting, ghostly darkness symbolizing the genocidal legacies of colonization. This colonial night represents the oppressive shadow cast by systemic violence, Christian imperialism, and the historical erasure of Indigenous identities and cultural practices. It is a place where the narrator confronts the lingering specters of intergenerational trauma and institutionalized abuse.

In contrast, the novel also depicts the "shamanic night," a luminous and transformative space of erotic pleasure and connection with nonhuman entities. Within this shamanic realm, the narrator reclaims her ancestral ties to the land and sky, breaking free from the colonial narratives imposed upon her. In a particularly striking moment, Tagaq imagines the Northern Lights as an erotic lover—a sensual, life-giving force that aids the narrator in reconnecting with her shamanic heritage. This intimate relationship with the Northern Lights becomes a source of healing and renewal, enabling the narrator to overcome the collective shame and violence instilled by Christian imperialism. By portraying the Northern Lights as an erotic Other that gives birth to miraculous forms of life, Tagaq decolonizes the Arctic night, revealing the transformative potential within Indigenous stories of the night sky and the capacity of Indigenous erotics to heal, resist, and imagine new futures rooted in cosmological connections.

The Colonial Night

According to Robert Shaw (2014), nighttime heightens the vulnerabilities of home, opening the self to encounters with ambivalence and otherness that threaten one's emotional and affective well-being. In *Split Tooth*, the domestic Other that corrupts the home is depicted as the colonial night—an intrusive, phantasmagoric force where the ghosts of past imperial harms turn the home into a space of fear, entrapment, and isolation. For example, the novel begins by plunging the reader into the narrator's harrowing world of persistent and brutal domestic violence. As the narrator recounts in the chilling opening scene:

> The drunks came home rowdier than usual one night, so we opted for the closet. We giggle nervously as the yelling begins. Become silent when the thumping starts. The whole house shakes. Women are screaming, but that sound is overtaken by the sound of things breaking. Wet sounds of flesh breaking and dry sounds of wood snapping, or is that bone?

Throughout *Split Tooth*, the nocturnal home is depicted as a site of profound vulnerability, standing in stark contrast to the ideals of white domesticity, which are often associated with safety, stability, and security. Instead of embodying these comforting qualities, the nocturnal home in the novel becomes a space where the legacies of colonialism manifest in eruptive moments of violence, rape, rampant alcoholism, and neglect. Frequent descriptions of bare cupboards and flimsy "fake-wood panel" walls, alongside tragic poems about rape and child molestation, reveal the harsh realities of nocturnal violence for Northern Indigenous communities.

To convey the ineffable damage inflicted on Indigenous communities, Tagaq depicts the night through the eerie and the strange, invoking spectral and unseen forces to articulate the lingering impact of trauma that transcends generations. Malevolent forces lurk in the shadows, symbolizing both literal and metaphorical dangers that prey on the community's children. These sinister presences reflect the ongoing, pervasive harm of colonial violence, which operates not only through physical acts but also through psychological and spiritual disruption. The narrator's reflections during one of her family's many violent and drunken gatherings exemplify this haunting quality: "I look forward to the morning when everyone is back to the people I love," she writes. "There are evil beings in the room near the ceiling waiting to take over the drunken bodies, Grudges and Frustrations slobbering at the chance to return to human form, to violate, to kill, to fornicate; Old Spirits conniving and contriving more strife." Tagaq's use of spectral imagery here captures the cyclical and insidious nature of colonial violence. By personifying abstract forces like grudges and frustrations, the narrative gives shape to the ineffable pain endured by Indigenous communities, transforming it into something palpable yet otherworldly. The nocturnal home, then, becomes a battleground between the love and resilience of the narrator's family and the shadowy, malevolent forces born from colonial exploitation. This duality illustrates how the impacts of colonialism are not confined to history but are embedded in the everyday realities of Indigenous life, where the night reveals both the scars of trauma and the potential for survival.

Through a wide range of uncanny passages, Tagaq illustrates how the night becomes a crucial space-time for the entrenchment of colonialism, revealing the profound dissonance created by colonial narratives in Indigenous lives. In particular, the concept of temporal discrimination—how the narrator experiences the loss of the night's nurturing and harmonious qualities—plays a critical role in perpetuating the myth of "Indigenous deficiency." As Daniel Heath Justice (2018) observes, one of the most damaging Eurocentric narratives about Indigenous Peoples is the notion that their struggles stem from an inherent lack of character. This racist myth frames high levels of poverty, depression, and violence in Indigenous communities as the result of perceived deficiencies in morals, culture, or language, rather than as consequences of systemic racism and colonial oppression. Furthermore, as Sarah Best explains, Western authorities have historically relied on the so-called "civilizing" forces of colonialism and Christianity to address these perceived deficiencies and "modernize" Indigenous ways of life. As Best (2023) writes:

> These forces constitute a direct attack on Indigenous-grounded normativity, as they attempt to sever the connections between Indigenous bodies and their lands, tearing apart the political systems and knowledges that are rooted in these relationships. This assault on Indigenous ways of life is what Simpson calls "expansive dispossession"—the ongoing seizure of Indigenous lands and erasure of Indigenous bodies as a means of marginalizing the political systems housed within them [...] Because of this expansive dispossession, many came to see Indigenous peoples and nations as relics of the past, irrelevant to contemporary society (10).

In *Split Tooth*, Tagaq challenges the myth of Indigenous deficiency by revealing how colonial systems infiltrate the darkness, dispossessing Indigenous Peoples of the capacity to transform the night into a time for community building and cultural empowerment. In the novel, nocturnal violence arises, not from a lack of moral character but a historical process involving a host of racist, neglectful, and marginalizing institutions. The residential school system, the imposition of Christian doctrine, the erasure of Indigenous language and culture, and the capitalistic extraction of Indigenous lands, it is these pathologies of colonialism that rob the Arctic night of its wonder, the ability to transform the home into what Lorimer calls an "emotional hearth" (Lorimer, 2005). Reflecting on the historical roots of the colonial night, the narrator states:

> My mother was a child of transition, government relocation, the shift into capitalism, and the moulting of the Shaman skin led to the generation of Christian rules, blind faith, and shame. Christians seem to love shame. Shame your body, your soul, your actions and inactions, put a cork in all of your holes and choke on the light of God.

To challenge the myth of deficiency, Tagaq employs a second nocturnal aesthetic, most vividly illustrated through the narrator's fantastical erotic encounter with the Northern Lights. Unlike the colonial night, where Christian shame haunts the home and enforces alienation, the starry night provides a space of temporal sovereignty, enabling the narrator to reconnect with her shamanic roots and embark on a journey of healing. As Sarah Best (2023) explains, "Temporal sovereignty is fundamentally intertwined with bodily and spatial sovereignty, and the embodied remembering that [...] allows for the colonial past to be re-enacted and re-written in the present, so that cultural healing and resurgence may occur through a continuity with rather than a severing from the past" (p. 6).

In *Split Tooth*, this reclamation of temporal sovereignty becomes inseparable from the narrator's sensual encounter with the Northern Lights, which she experiences as an erotic Other. By transcending the boundaries of human and nonhuman eros, the narrator opens a liminal space where she can both reclaim her body as a site of joy and agency, breaking free from the shame imposed by Christian doctrines, and reconnect with the cosmic rhythms and ancestral knowledge disrupted by colonial violence. This experience of eros as politically transformative resonates with Audre Lorde's conceptualization of eros as a force of transgression. For Lorde, erotic pleasure is not limited to sexual experience; it is a profound capacity to translate embodied joy into social and political change. Eros, as Lorde writes, is a source of power and knowledge that resists the oppression of patriarchal, racist hierarchies. It fosters care, connection, and creativity, expanding the self's capacity to imagine and pursue new possibilities. As Nikki Young (2012) explains, "Lorde's erotic innovation [...] has established itself as a political, social, and academic tool of deconstruction, subversion, and imagination" (p. 301).

For many Indigenous scholars, Audre Lorde's call to harness the power of eros resonates deeply with the cultivation of relational ethics of care, where erotic pleasure fosters and sustains more-than-human connections with the world. As Daniel Heath Justice (2008) writes, "To take joy in our bodies, and those bodies in relation to others, is to strike out against five hundred-plus years of disregard, disrespect, and dismissal" (p. 103). This relationality lies at the core of Indigenous erotics, emphasizing the interconnectedness of all beings and the role of joy and care in restoring and maintaining these relationships. Turtle Mountain Chippewa scholar Melissa Nelson (2017) highlights that, for many Indigenous women, the purpose of erotic literature is to enhance ecological relationships and kinships between humans and nonhumans. Nelson's perspective redefines eros as an eco-centric force, one that transcends Western settler understandings of sexuality focused on bodily pleasures or human-centered interactions. Instead, Indigenous erotics embraces a holistic vision of relationships that extend to the living and the dead, the material and the immaterial, and across all dimensions of time. It encompasses not only the immediacy of the present but also the memories of ancestral kin and the potential of future generations. Akiwenzie-Damm also notes that much of Indigenous erotic literature centers on life-affirming relationships with nature and the bonds of care that permeate all existence. Through this lens, erotic pleasure becomes an act of reclamation and resurgence, one that counters colonial narratives of shame and detachment by reaffirming the sacred and interconnected nature of all life.

While in *Split Tooth* the narrator experiences many more-than-human erotic encounters, the most transformative occurs during her sensual union with the Northern Lights, an experience that reclaims the Arctic night as a site of profound healing, renewal, and cosmological connection. In Inuit tradition, the Northern Lights are understood as the dancing souls of the departed, serving as guides and protectors for the living. This interpretation positions the Lights as both ancestral presences and cosmic forces, bridging the material and spiritual worlds. One night, seeking refuge from the violence and chaos of her parents' drunken party, the narrator ventures alone onto the sea ice. There, beneath the vast expanse of the Arctic night, she enters an otherworldly erotic encounter with the Northern Lights. As she gazes at the sky, she describes seeing "a sliver morphing into a great curtain of movement that pulsates from east to west, parallel to my form on the ice. The lights become bolder and grow closer. They seem curious, drawn by the sound of flesh and my meagre offering of spirit." The Lights, depicted as sentient and inquisitive, approach her with a more-than-human agency, establishing an intimate and reciprocal connection.

The union becomes profoundly physical and spiritual when the narrator falls beneath the ice, a symbolic moment of vulnerability and surrender. As the icy waters engulf her, the Northern Lights envelop her body, entering her with shards of luminous energy. This moment is at once erotic and transformative, as the light inflicts both pain and healing. She recounts:

> The splitting continues down my belly, lighting up my liver and excavating my bladder. An impossible column of green light simultaneously impales my vagina and anus. My clit explodes and I am split in two from head to toe as the light from my throat joins the light in my womb and begins to make a giant fluid figure eight in my body.

Here Tagaq portrays the Lights as a force of creation and destruction, splitting the narrator apart while simultaneously reconfiguring her being. The use of fluid, cyclical imagery—such as the figure eight—symbolizes infinite renewal and continuity, evoking ancestral rhythms disrupted by colonial violence. The Northern Lights' entry into her body becomes an act of reclamation, healing her wounds while re-establishing her connection to the cosmos and her shamanic heritage.

During her erotic encounter with the Northern Lights, the narrator experiences a nonlinear sense of time that begins to heal her colonial wounds. This moment stands in stark contrast to the hierarchical, linear temporality imposed by colonial rule. Instead, the Northern Lights impregnate the narrator with a sense of temporal thickness—a non-hierarchical understanding of time that connects her with her shamanic heritage and cosmic kin. The narrator recounts:

> The Northern Lights grow larger still and begin to morph into faces, blurry, omnipotent, healing and death-dealing. They sharpen and I see Aunties and Great-grandmothers. I see Ancestors and future children; the young ones are just developing and preparing their spirits for the next rotation of Earth Journey. It takes millennia to return to Earth after we die. I weep at the majesty of our ancestors and give thanks for the opportunity to witness them.

In this visionary moment, the narrator encounters time as a cyclical and interconnected continuum, where past, present, and future overlap. Ancestors and unborn children coexist as active participants in a shared cosmic journey, emphasizing a temporality deeply rooted in relationality, continuity, and healing.

As Akiwenzie-Damm (2003) notes, the purpose of Indigenous erotic writing is to provide "medicine" that helps heal the often-forgotten wounds of colonial harm. In *Split Tooth*, this healing medicine emerges from the coupling of eros and maternal care. The Northern Lights' insemination of the narrator carries the dual symbolism of creation and restoration, reconnecting her with a community of past and future kin. As the narrator describes later in the novel, her babies embody this cyclical time, representing both her ancestors and future generations. "Through my babies," she reflects:

> I wordlessly speak with the past; through baby boy, I speak with a quiet and serene old man that keeps an eye on the horizon to make sure the world spins properly on its axis. Through baby girl, I speak to a giant female wolf that stalks the periphery of our territory to detect predators. Both are silent, but who needs words to speak when all is already known?

This blending of eros and maternal care positions the narrator's relationship with her children as a conduit for intergenerational communication and cosmological balance. Her children are not merely offspring but embodied connections to ancestral wisdom and future guardianship, affirming a relational understanding of time that resists colonial erasures.

Throughout the latter part of *Split Tooth*, the narrator undergoes a profound transformation, using her erotic encounter with the Northern Lights to reclaim her maternal home as a site of decolonization. As Qwo-Li Driskill (2016) explains, decolonization involves the act of reclaiming "our lives, our languages, our lands, our song, our plants, our memories, our bodies" (pp. 169–170). In this light, the narrator's journey shifts from the nocturnal harm and violence that dominate the first half of the novel to a process of recovery and empowerment following her miraculous impregnation by the Northern Lights. The narrator's transformation is evident in her newfound courage and resilience. She no longer exhibits timidity at school, standing up to her bullies with assertiveness and strength. The novel also implies that the sexual abuse she endured has ended, as her maternal instincts and connection to her shamanic roots grant her the power to reclaim her body and spirit. This process of decolonization allows her to redefine the domestic sphere—not as a site of harm but as a place of strength, healing, and cultural continuity. The narrator conveys this transformation through one of the novel's many poetic celebrations of her fearlessness. She writes:

> Bare my Teeth
> One Slavia String
> One tongue
> Cannot speak of the
> fight that comes from survival
> Touch my children
> And my teeth welcome your windpipe

Utter the name
And be crushed by leg
grown strong from
holding up weight
by thigh that carries
rocks and urgent gait
I will hunch my shoulders and wait
class sharpened
teeth agape

Although *Split Tooth* presents two distinct experiences of darkness—the colonial night and the ancestral night of myth and legend—describing the narrator's transformation in linear terms risks missing a key element of her journey: the nonlinear, cyclical entanglements with time that disrupt colonial narratives of linear temporality. In her analysis of the North, Margaret Atwood observes that many white Canadian writers are drawn to the notion that indigeneity allows one the opportunity to step back in time and discover an authentic self in communion with "pure" wilderness. This romanticized framework assumes a linear progression of history, where nature exists as an unchanging backdrop to human self-discovery. Similarly, Emile Cameron critiques settler narratives for frequently employing ghosts and ghouls to evoke a generalized sense of history within a framework of linearity and succession. Cameron (2008) explains, "The Aboriginal ghost has been utilized to evoke a generalized sense of history in the Canadian landscape, but always within a framework of linearity and succession. It is assumed that Aboriginal ghosts are all that remains of the 'disappearing Indian' and that settler Canadians have inherited this rich land from those who have now 'passed'" (p. 384).

Split Tooth challenges these colonial notions of time and the supernatural by reframing myths, spirits, and ancestral connections as living and active forces that resist erasure. For many Indigenous writers, fantastical myths about the past are not relics of a bygone era; they serve as pathways toward future forms of decolonized sociability and cultural resurgence. As Warren Cariou (2006) notes:

> Native writers do represent spirits in their work [...] it is just that these spirits are not necessarily figures of uncanny terror. They may be malevolent beings [...] but they may also be figures of healing, ceremony, or political action. Or they may simply be ancestors. And while many such spirits do seem to address the transgressions of the colonial past, they usually do so as part of a call for some kind of redress or change in the present. (p. 730)

In *Split Tooth*, spirits and other supernatural beings function as agents of transformation and healing rather than mere vestiges of a "disappearing" past. The narrator's erotic encounter with the Northern Lights embodies this sense of time, as it blurs temporal boundaries and reconfigures her relationship with time. The Lights enable her to connect with ancestors and future generations simultaneously, emphasizing a relational temporality that resists the linear, extractive frameworks of settler colonialism. This cyclical understanding of time positions myths and legends not as static stories about a distant past but as dynamic forces that guide the narrator toward decolonial futures. As such, *Split Tooth* can be seen as an example of what Grace Dillon (2012) describes as "Native slipstream"—a temporal framework common in many Indigenous narratives where "pasts, presents, and futures [...] flow together like currents in a navigable stream" (p. 10). Rather than a static backdrop, the night becomes what Karen Barad (2017) terms "material reconfiguration of spacetimematterings," a process of becoming that attempts "to do justice for the devastation wrought and to produce new openings, new possible histories, ultimately facilitating persistence and survival" (p. 76). In this sense, the narrator's encounters with the night—such as her erotic union with the Northern Lights—become acts of reparation and renewal, where ancestral knowledge and future potential converge in the present moment to facilitate persistence and survival.

Understood another way, in *Split Tooth* the Arctic night emerges as a space for the transmission of Qaujimajatuqangit (IQ), the oral traditions and histories passed down through generations to Inuit Elders before the imposition of residential schools. Rooted in "what the Inuit have known for a very long time," IQ reflects "the Inuit way of doing things: the past, present, and future knowledge, experience, and values of Inuit society" (Martin, 2012). This worldview emphasizes the interconnectedness of time, space, and community, positioning the night as a vital realm for cultural continuity and renewal. As many night scholars have observed, darkness has long been recognized as a period of creative rejuvenation, when stories about nature, society, and survival are shared with younger generations. Within Inuit culture, these wonder-filled narratives offer not only practical guidance for understanding the natural world but also profound insights into cosmology and spirituality. In this context, *Split Tooth* highlights how the Arctic night, as a space for the transmission of IQ, resists the linear and extractive temporality of settler colonialism. Through the transformative powers of eros, it reclaims darkness as a site of wonder, renewal, and cultural resilience, emphasizing its importance for shaping decolonial futures.

Myth Three: Victimhood, Rural Crime, and the Arctic Night

Since 2014, HBO's true crime series *True Detective* has garnered critical acclaim for its compelling and visually striking portrayals of detectives grappling with deeply disturbing cases involving serial killers, child rapists, and missing Indigenous women. Like the crime-based media of the past, *True Detective* uses the urban night as a powerful backdrop to explore themes of moral decay, political corruption, and social fragmentation. The series thus fits nicely within a broader cultural framework that associates the urban night with transgression, anxiety, and the darker undercurrents of modern life. As Will Straw (2005) observes, since the 1950s, mass media have consistently drawn on the urban night to represent crime and its detection. Film noir, for example, famously depicted foggy streets, shadowy alleyways, and dimly lit nightclubs as spaces where moral and social boundaries dissolve, providing a visual lexicon for urban transgression. Similarly, the lurid covers of True Crime magazines dramatized criminality and sin, reinforcing the association between the urban night and narratives of deviance and disorder. Over time, this media repertoire of urban signs—including foggy streets, fedora hats, darkened casinos, and neon-lit bars—came to symbolize more than just crime; they "pulled together anxieties over urban decay, Cold War concerns about national moral weakness, newly intrusive coverage of the private lives of celebrities, and shifts in the social acceptability of certain classes of sexual imagery and behaviour" (9).

In 2024, HBO released *Night Country*, a new installment in the *True Detective* anthology series set in Alaska during the long, polar night. By choosing this rural nighttime setting, *Night Country* departed from the classic urban visuals traditionally associated with crime dramas, offering fresh and creative aesthetic approaches to the genre. Most notably, the series became the first prime-time crime drama to feature a female Indigenous detective in a leading role, marking a significant shift in how such narratives engage with race, gender, and representation. Since the golden age of prime-time television in the 2000s, crime dramas have increasingly expanded their representation of race and gender by diversifying the roles of lead detectives. Acclaimed series like *Mare of Easttown*, *Broadchurch*, *The Killing*, *The Fall*, and *Happy Valley* have prominently featured women as lead investigators, placing them at the forefront of narratives that confront societal breakdowns, moral decay, and systemic failures, often depicted against urban backdrops. *Night Country* continues this trend by featuring two female detectives in leading roles, but it goes a step further by introducing a female Indigenous detective, thus broadening the scope of representation in meaningful ways.

This casting choice is especially significant given the ongoing crisis of missing and murdered Indigenous women (MMIW), a devastating issue that has historically received minimal attention in mainstream media. The inclusion of an Indigenous detective offers a much-needed "insider" perspective, challenging the pervasive outsider narratives that often frame Indigenous communities through the lens of exoticism, victimhood, or criminality. By centering an Indigenous woman as both a protagonist and a moral agent, *Night Country* confronts the systemic failures and colonial legacies that perpetuate violence against Indigenous women, while also offering a vision of resilience, expertise, and agency.

The story of *Night Country* unfolds around the mysterious and brutal murder of a group of white geologists conducting research near the communal lands of the Iñupiat. As the investigation progresses, the narrative centers on Evangeline, a troubled Indigenous detective who becomes convinced that these murders are connected to the deaths and disappearances of local Indigenous women. Her relentless pursuit of justice not only drives the story but also offers a rare and powerful lens through which mainstream media can explore the ongoing violence inflicted on Indigenous communities—a crisis often overlooked or marginalized in public discourse. Historically, Indigenous characters in mainstream media have been constrained by reductive and harmful stereotypes, such as the "simple Indian" or the "spiritual guide." These representations often romanticize Indigenous Peoples as having a "natural" affinity with nature, casting them as either primitive relics of the past or noble protectors of the environment, existing primarily to provide lessons or warnings for Western societies. Such portrayals serve to flatten Indigenous identities, erasing their lived realities and perpetuating colonial narratives of otherness.

In *Night Country*, the setting of the long polar night becomes a potent backdrop for challenging these reductive tropes and offering a decolonized representation of Indigenous Peoples. Rather than leaning on stereotypes, the series presents Evangeline as a multidimensional character—flawed, resilient, and deeply connected to her community and culture. Her push for justice is not just a personal crusade; it is an act of resistance against the systemic neglect and colonial violence that have long endangered Indigenous lives and erased their stories. As Agata Lulkowska writes:

> True Detective offers a nuanced portrays of the Iñupiat. They are not "bad" nor they are "good"—they are ordinary people just like everyone else, with their own problems and valuable heritage. The show's creators have gone beyond cheap and overused stereotypes to allow for a more realistic depiction of contemporary indigenous lives: one which is not trapped in the past but still benefits from traditional values.

The polar night, with its endless darkness, amplifies the show's exploration of obscured truths and systemic failures. Throughout the series, darkness becomes a metaphor for the erasure of Indigenous voices and experiences, as well as a space for reclaiming visibility and agency. By situating the crimes against Indigenous women alongside the murders of white geologists, *Night Country* highlights the stark disparities in how society values and investigates these lives, critiquing the historical devaluation of Indigenous lives and communities. Moreover, *Night Country* does not romanticize Evangeline's connection to the land or her cultural heritage. Instead, it portrays her relationships with her community, culture, and environment as complex and lived realities. Her knowledge of Iñupiat traditions and her awareness of colonial harms inform her approach to the investigation, but they do not define her as a one-dimensional archetype. This nuanced depiction allows *Night Country* to address colonial harms without reducing Indigenous identity to a set of stereotypes.

In addition to decolonizing the night through its portrayal of Evangeline, *Night Country* also foregrounds a powerful community of Indigenous women who band together to confront systemic injustices, including police brutality and environmental destruction. By doing so, the show challenges both historical and contemporary narratives that have long marginalized Indigenous women's agency and resistance. As mentioned earlier, for many early white settlers, the Arctic night was perceived as a hostile and chaotic force, an unruly wilderness that could only be subdued by the courage and fortitude of resilient men. In *Night Country*, this perception is subverted entirely. Rather than depicting Indigenous Peoples as struggling against the harsh elements of the polar night, the show positions white male geologists as victims of its dangers. For example, in the opening episode, the geologists are discovered frozen to death, their bodies grotesquely twisted in the snow. Initially, viewers are led to believe their deaths might be caused by a mysterious Arctic force or a mental disturbance brought on by the long polar night. As the narrative unfolds, however, it becomes clear that their deaths are neither accidental nor inexplicable. Rather, their deaths were the calculated actions of a group of Indigenous women seeking justice for the harm inflicted on their land and people. As the viewer learns near the end of the series, the geologists had been deliberately poisoning the local water supply, disregarding the devastating effects on the surrounding community. To seek justice against these colonial activities, the women brutally murder them, making it look like a case of polar madness. By attributing justice not to a nameless Arctic entity but to the resilience and determination of Indigenous women, *Night Country* thus critiques the ongoing colonial violence inflicted on Indigenous communities, particularly in the form of environmental exploitation. Indeed, the women's calculated actions serve as a stark contrast to the historical invisibility of Indigenous women in mainstream media and their stereotypical portrayal as passive victims. Instead, the show celebrates the women's courage and collective power, as their special brand of decolonial justice not only exposes the failures of colonial institutions to protect Indigenous lives and lands but also highlights the creative ways in which Indigenous communities can actively resist recurring colonial harms.

Like *Nalujuk Night* and *Split Tooth*, *Night Country* resists framing the night in terms of the polarizing binary found in many Western discourses about darkness. The night is not simply an inhospitable space-time containing terrifying evils, nor is it a cumbersome testing ground for white settlers to prove their national pride or robust manliness. Instead, *Night Country* uses the eerie and seemingly endless darkness of the arctic night—to explore themes of disappearance, marginalization, justice, and the resilience of the tight-knit communities that call the Arctic home. By intertwining these aesthetic and narrative elements with the urgent issue of MMIW, *Night Country* not only revitalizes the crime drama genre but also takes significant steps toward decolonizing it, offering a platform for underrepresented voices that address the intersection of race, gender, and colonial violence in ways that challenge traditional crime narratives.

Conclusion

Since the advent of mass electrification, the global North has persistently sought to push back and domesticate darkness, radically reshaping nighttime landscapes by aligning them with the demands of productivity and surveillance. While urban initiatives, such as the rise of night mayors who advocate for preserving the cultural and ecological value of the night, signal a growing awareness of the consequences of light pollution, darkness continues to diminish. Given this sorry state, it may be tempting to imagine that rural areas, including the so-called "remoteness" of the Arctic, provide a final refuge from the colonization of the night. This belief, however, overlooks the encroachment of modern technologies, such as satellite constellations and industrial developments, that increasingly disrupt even the most isolated regions. As Atwood cautions:

> But the bad news is coming in: the North is not endless. It is not vast and strong and capable of devouring and digesting all the human dirt thrown its way [...] The edifice of Northern imagery we've been discussing in these lectures was erected on a reality; if that reality ceases to exist, the imagery, too, will cease to have any resonance or meaning, except as a

> sort of indecipherable hieroglyphic. The North will be neither female nor male, neither fearful nor health-giving, because it will be dead. The Earth, like trees, dies from the top down. The things that are killing the North will kill, if left unchecked, everything else.

Thus, while many ideological understandings of the polar night presume that the Arctic is immune to the forces of light pollution and artificial illumination, in reality, the North is subject to the same resource extraction industries, military operations, and communication infrastructures that continue to disrupt urban places by overpowering them with artificial illumination. Moreover, the framing of the Arctic as a "remote" or "untouched" wilderness reflects colonial assumptions about land and space. Framed within a postcolonial perspective, such narratives obscure the lived realities of Arctic communities, who actively inhabit and shape their environments. For many Indigenous Peoples, darkness is not an absence or void but a rich and dynamic presence, integral to their cosmologies, oral traditions, and ways of life. The diminishing of darkness, therefore, represents more than an ecological loss; it is also a cultural and spiritual erosion, disrupting Indigenous relationships with the land, the sky, and their ancestral knowledge.

In this context, the preservation of darkness must be understood not simply as an environmental issue but as a broader act of resistance against the colonization of time, space, and culture. It requires challenging the economic imperatives and technological developments that continue to erase the night, while also honoring the wisdom and practices of those who have long thrived in harmony with its rhythms. The Arctic night, far from being a passive backdrop, serves as a reminder of the vital importance of darkness—not only as a natural phenomenon but as a space for reflection, creativity, and connection.

Conclusion

RECLAIMING THE MEDIATED NIGHT

As the relentless glow of artificial illumination pushes natural darkness further into the recesses of our collective memory, the night sky, once a universal canvas for human wonder, storytelling, and scientific inquiry, has become an increasingly scarce resource. In *Media and the Myth of the Pristine Night*, I examine not only the physical loss of darkness but also the complex cultural and technological mediations that shape our understanding of what the night is and what darkness means in an era defined by urbanization, technological saturation, and the looming specter of the Anthropocene. While many of these concerns have been exemplified by the rise of the "night mayor," a figure symbolizing the growing recognition of the urban night as a distinct economic, social, and political domain requiring dedicated governance, another powerful, pervasive, and ultimately problematic counter-narrative has emerged: the myth of the pristine night. This myth, deeply ingrained in Western environmental thought and propagated through various media forms, posits "true" darkness as an untouched, pretechnological wilderness found only in remote rural landscapes, a sanctuary untainted by the perceived ills of modernity and human intervention.

Throughout the preceding chapters, I have critically examined this myth, arguing that the idealization of pristine darkness is not merely a nostalgic yearning but a complex cultural technology that obscures more than it reveals. It perpetuates a false dichotomy between nature and culture, urban and rural, technology and authenticity, hindering a more nuanced and effective engagement with the multifaceted challenges and opportunities presented by darkness in the contemporary world. By analyzing a diverse array of media—from the technologically enhanced gaze of nocturnal nature documentaries and the romanticized vistas of astro-tourism posters to the digital erasure in astrophotography, the immersive environments of interactive art, and the decolonial narratives of Indigenous media—this book has sought to dismantle the pristine myth and advocate for a more critical, interconnected, and historically grounded understanding of the night.

Moving beyond the myth of the pristine requires embracing a more nuanced and critical understanding of darkness in all its forms. This involves recognizing that technological mediations are crucial for our understanding of nature. As explored in Chapter One, new technologies, such as low-light and thermal cameras, don't just reveal "hidden" nature; they foreground technological mediation itself, presenting viewers with strange, hybrid depictions of the night that challenge simplistic notions of naturalism. These technologies reveal the "weirdness" of nocturnal life and the unsettling intrusions of the wild into the urban (and vice-versa), forcing a confrontation with the messy entanglements of ecosystems rather than retreating into idealized separation.

The allure of the pristine is powerful, rooted in a long history of Romantic ideals that sought solace and spiritual renewal in "untouched" wilderness as an antidote to the perceived corruptions of industrial society. As explored in Chapter Two through Tyler Nordgren's *Half the Park is After Dark* poster series, this legacy persists in contemporary astro-tourism. Nordgren's evocative imagery, drawing on the aesthetics of nineteenth-century landscape art and frontier nostalgia, frames Dark Sky Parks as sacred refuges where visitors can encounter the astronomical sublime—a timeless, ancient cosmos unsullied by modernity. The Milky Way becomes a "window to the universe," a source of "wordless worship," connecting viewers to a primordial past. However, as William Cronon compellingly argued regarding the myth of wilderness, this romanticization represents a "flight from history." Nordgren's posters, while beautiful, construct a de-historicized and domesticated sublime, erasing the complexities and contradictions inherent in seeking pristine experiences. They conveniently omit the technological infrastructure (roads, lodges, transportation) that enable such tourism, mirroring the historical development of national parks themselves, which, as Richard Grusin demonstrated, were co-produced by tourism technologies. More significantly, in the context of the night sky, this aesthetic of purity actively conceals the ongoing technological transformations occurring above, most notably the proliferation of satellite constellations whose trails increasingly "pollute" even the darkest skies. By fetishizing an unchanging, ancient night, such representations foster escapism rather than critical engagement with the systemic drivers of light pollution, including the very space technologies reshaping the celestial sphere. Beauty, framed through this nostalgic and exclusionary lens, proves insufficient to save the starry night; it merely papers over the cracks in a rapidly changing reality.

The active erasure of technological reality was further explored in Chapter Three, focusing on the visual politics of satellite trails in astrophotography. Here, the pristine myth manifests not through romantic idealization but through technological remediation. Satellite trails, artifacts of the burgeoning satellite internet industry and the neoliberal "race to space," are framed by many in the astronomical community as "visual pollutants," matter out of place that contaminates the desired aesthetic of an unblemished, ancestral sky. Advanced software and AI tools are employed to digitally remove these trails, restoring the image to a state of perceived purity. While scientifically necessary for data integrity in some contexts, this practice of digital erasure functions as a form of Anthropocene visuality. It cleanses the visual world of any evidence of human impact, normalizing the infrastructural colonization of space and obscuring the political and ecological consequences of unchecked satellite deployment and the mounting crisis of space debris. This approach contrasts sharply with the counter-visual strategies employed by artists like Trevor Paglen. In projects like *The Last Pictures* and *Orbital Reflector*, Paglen actively foregrounds the material and political realities of space infrastructure, challenging the notion of space as an empty frontier and exposing it as a contested zone shaped by corporate interests, surveillance, and the unsettling temporal paradox of creating "eternal" technological waste through planned obsolescence. His art resists the depoliticizing impulse of the pristine, urging viewers to confront the entanglements of technology, capitalism, governance, and the environment that define our relationship with the contemporary night sky.

While the critique of the pristine often focuses on the idealization of natural darkness, Chapter Four shifted the focus to the potential of artificial darkness, particularly within the context of urban interactive art installations by the collective teamLab. Building on the legacy of the Light and Space movement and figures like James Turrell, teamLab utilizes technologically mediated darkness not as a void, but as an active aesthetic element. In immersive environments like Borderless or The Infinite Crystal Universe, darkness becomes a canvas for dynamic light projections that respond to visitor interaction. These installations evoke the wonder and awe often associated with natural stargazing but do so within accessible urban settings. Crucially, teamLab's work challenges the binary opposition between natural authenticity and artificial simulation. By creating "ultrasubjective spaces" where viewers become co-creators, dissolving the traditional distance between observer and artwork, teamLab fosters social intimacy and connection. Darkness, in these contexts, enhances sensory perception (particularly touch), reduces self-consciousness, and promotes a sense of shared experience and egalitarian participation, echoing the social potential observed in urban light festivals. This suggests that an appreciation for darkness need not rely solely on retreating to remote wilderness. Urban environments, through thoughtful design and artistic intervention, can cultivate a positive relationship with darkness, offering alternative pathways for conservation advocacy that embrace technology and collective experience rather than rejecting them in pursuit of an elusive purity.

The limitations and colonial underpinnings of the pristine myth become starkly apparent when viewed through the lens of Indigenous experiences and knowledge systems, as explored in Chapter Five. The concept of astro-colonization underscores how the technological appropriation of the night sky, particularly through the proliferation of satellites, poses a threat to Indigenous astronomical traditions, which are vital components of cultural identity, spirituality, navigation, and storytelling. Western narratives have often depicted the Arctic night, particularly the long polar night, through colonial myths of harshness, isolation, and primitivism, associating darkness with fear, mental anguish, and the "uncivilized." Indigenous media, however, offers powerful counter-narratives that decolonize the night. Jennie Williams' Nalujuk Night portrays the polar night not as a time of isolation but as a vibrant period for communal ritual, storytelling, and social cohesion, where darkness facilitates shared experience and the transmission of cultural knowledge. Tanya Tagaq's novel *Split Tooth* masterfully contrasts the colonial night—a space haunted by the trauma of residential schools, violence, and Christian shame—with the shamanic night. In this latter space, the narrator engages in an erotic, transformative encounter with the Northern Lights, reclaiming her body, connecting with ancestral and future kin, and accessing a cyclical, relational temporality that resists colonial linearity. This Indigenous eroticism, as theorized by scholars like Audre Lorde and Daniel Heath Justice, becomes a source of healing, resilience, and political resistance. Finally, the HBO series *True Detective: Night Country*, by centering on an Iñupiat detective investigating crimes against Indigenous women during the polar night, subverts stereotypes of Indigenous victimhood. It portrays Indigenous characters with complexity and agency, highlighting their resilience and resistance against systemic violence and environmental exploitation perpetrated by colonial forces (represented by the polluting mine). Together, these works demonstrate that for many Indigenous cultures, darkness is not a void to be feared or conquered, but a profound source of knowledge, creativity, connection, healing, and resistance—a perspective fundamentally incompatible with the simplistic, often exclusionary, myth of the pristine.

This exploration across diverse media landscapes reveals that the pristine night is less a reflection of reality and more a product of specific cultural anxieties, historical legacies, and technological mediations. The desire to preserve a pure, untouched darkness often stems from a discomfort with modernity, technology, and the complex entanglements of human activity with the environment. Yet, as this book has argued, retreating into this myth is counterproductive. It prevents us from acknowledging the ways humans have always mediated the night, from the first campfires to the latest satellite networks. It obscures the deep interconnectedness of rural and urban spaces, where the glow of cities impacts remote skies and the infrastructure enabling rural connectivity (like satellites) contributes to global light pollution. It risks alienating urban populations, who constitute the majority of the world, by suggesting that authentic experiences with darkness are only available through escape. And, perhaps most critically, it often perpetuates colonial modes of thinking that devalue nonWestern ways of knowing and erase the histories and ongoing presence of Indigenous peoples whose relationships with the night are rich, complex, and vital.

Ultimately, reclaiming the night—both rural and urban—is not about returning to an imagined, unmediated past. It is about critically engaging with the present, acknowledging the complex interplay of light and dark, nature and technology, culture and politics that defines our contemporary experience. It requires moving beyond the seductive but limiting binary of the pristine versus the polluted, the natural versus the artificial. The night, like the environment itself, is not static or separate; it is a dynamic, relational, and deeply mediated space-time. Preserving its value—whether for scientific observation, cultural heritage, ecological health, or simple human wonder—demands that we confront its complexities head-on, armed with critical awareness, technological understanding, and a commitment to more inclusive and historically conscious narratives. The challenge lies not in escaping modernity to find darkness, but in learning to navigate the mediated darkness we inhabit, fostering a relationship with the night that is both appreciative of its profound beauty and cognizant of the forces that continue to shape its future. Only by unveiling the myths that obscure our vision can we hope to foster a truly sustainable and equitable relationship with the darkness that surrounds us.

BIBLIOGRAPHY

Abram, S. 2003. "Gazing on Rurality." In: Cloke, P. ed. *Country Visions*. Harlow: Pearson, pp. 32–48.

Akiwenzie-Damm, K. 2003. *Without Reservation: Indigenous Erotica*. Cape Croker Reserve: Kegedonce.

Albers, P.C. and James, W.R. 1988. "Travel Photography: A Methodological Approach." *Annals of Tourism Research*, 15(1), pp. 134–158.

Alves, T. 2007. "Art, Light and Landscape New Agendas for Urban Development." *European Planning Studies*, 15(9), pp. 1247–1260.

Arnheim, R. 2020. *Art and Visual Perception*. 2nd Edition, reprint 2020 ed. Berkeley, CA: University of California Press.

Ashworth, J. 2023. "Increasing Light Pollution Is Drowning Out the Stars." *Natural History Museum*, 19 January. Available at: https://www.nhm.ac.uk/discover/news/2023/january/increasing-light-pollution-drowning-out-stars.html#:~:text=The%20stars%20are%20vanishing%20before,brighter%20each%20year%20on%20average [Accessed 5 June 2024].

Atwood, M. 1995. *Strange Things: The Malevolent North in Canadian Literature*. Clarendon Press. Kindle Edition.

Aufderheide, P. 2007. *Documentary Film: A Very Short History*. Oxford: Oxford University Press. Kindle Edition.

Barad, K. 2012. "On Touching – the Inhuman That Therefore I Am." *Differences (Bloomington, Ind.)*, 23(3), pp. 206–223. https://doi.org/10.1215/10407391-1892943

Barad, K. 2017. "Troubling Time/s and Ecologies of Nothingness: Re-turning, Re-membering, and Facing the Incalculable." *New Formations*, 92, pp. 56–86.

Barney, D. n.d. "Autonomous Agriculture?" *HELIOTROPE*. Available at: https://www.heliotropejournal.net/helio/autonomous-agriculture [Accessed 5 June 2024].

Barthes, R. 1999. "The Rhetoric of the Image." In: Evans, Jessica, ed. *Visual Culture: The Reader*. London: Sage Publications, pp. 33–40.

Bateson, G. 1972. *Steps to an Ecology of Mind*. First Ballantine Books Edition. New York: Ballantine Books.

Beauregard, R.A. 2002. *Voices of Decline: The Postwar Fate of US Cities*. New York: Routledge.

Beauregard, R.A. 2003. "City of Superlatives." *City & Community*, 2(3), pp. 183–199.

Benjamin, W. 1999. "Little History of Photography." In: Jennings, M.W., Eiland, H. and Smith, G. eds. *Walter Benjamin: Selected Writings, vol. 2, 1927–1934*. Cambridge, MA: Belknap Press, pp. 507–530.

Benjamin, W. 2008. *The Work of Art in the Age of Its Technological Reproducibility, and Other Writings on Media*. Cambridge, MA: Belknap Press: An Imprint of Harvard University Press.

Berger, J. 2008. *Ways of Seeing.* London: Penguin Classics.

Best, S. 2023. "Time-Diffraction Stories: Inuit Qaujimajatuqangit and Temporal Sovereignty in The Journals of Knud Rasmussen and Split Tooth." *Synoptique*, 10(1), pp. 5–30.

Bigelow, B.A. 2023. "INTRODUCTION: Uncanny Ecologies." In: *Menacing Environments.* United States: University of Washington Press., pp. 1–27.

Blue Planet II. 2018. [Film] Directed by James Honeyborne. United Kingdom: Warner Bros.

Blundell, E., Schaffer, V. and Moyle, B.D. 2020. "Dark Sky Tourism and the Sustainability of Regional Tourism Destinations." *Tourism Recreation Research*, 45(4), pp. 549–556.

Bogard, P. 2014. *The End of Night: Searching for Natural Darkness in an Age of Artificial Light.* New York: Back Bay Books. Kindle Edition.

Bogost, I. 2012. *Alien Phenomenology, Or, What It's Like to Be a Thing.* Minneapolis: University of Minnesota Press. Kindle Edition.

Bogost, I. 2025. "We're All in 'Dark Mode' Now: How Light-on-black Became a Way of Life." *The Atlantic.* Available at: https://www.theatlantic.com/technology/archive/2025/01/rise-of-dark-mode-apps/681162/ [Accessed 5 June 2024].

Brodie, M. 2020. "Wild West' in Space: Astronomers Concerned New, Brighter Satellites Could Hinder Observations from Earth." Available at: https://fronterasdesk.org/content/1614247/wild-west-space-astronomers-concerned-new-brighter-satellites-could-hinder [Accessed 5 June 2024].

Brown, P.L. 2000. *Megaliths, Myths and Men: An Introduction to Astro-Archaeology.* Mineola, NY: Dover Publications.

Brox, J. 2010. *Brilliant: The Evolution of Artificial Light.* Boston: Houghton Mifflin Harcourt.

Bryant, L., Srnicek, N., & Harman, G. (Eds.). (2010). "Towards a Speculative Philosophy." In: *The Speculative Turn: Continental Materialism and Realism.* Melbourne, Re.press.

Bryant, L.R., Srnicek, N. and Harman, G. 2011. *The Speculative Turn: Continental Materialism and Realism.* Melbourne, Victoria, South Australia: re.press. Kindle Edition.

Burke, E. 2018. *The Works of Edmund Burke: Volume 1.* Berlin: Verlag. Kindle Edition.

Cameron, E. 2008. "Indigenous Spectrality and the Politics of Postcolonial Ghost Stories." *Cultural Geographies*, 15(3), pp. 383–393.

Caraveo, P. 2021. *Saving the Starry Night: Light Pollution and Its Effects on Science, Culture and Nature.* Cham: Springer.

Carey, J. 1989. *Communication as Culture: Essays on Media and Society.* Boston: Unwin Hyman.

Cariou, W. 2006. "Haunted Prairie: Aboriginal 'Ghosts' and the Spectres of Settlement." *University of Toronto Quarterly*, 75(2), pp. 727–734.

Castells, M. 1992. *The Informational City: Economic Restructuring and Urban Development.* Oxford: Wiley-Blackwell.

Chapman, L. n.d. "The Imaginary of Emptiness, Newness, and Rural Ontologies: A Reflection After Media Rurality." *HELIOTROPE.* Available at: https://www.heliotropejournal.net/helio/imaginary-of-emptiness [Accessed 5 June 2024].

Chris, C. 2006. *Watching Wildlife.* Minneapolis: University of Minnesota Press.

Collins, K. 2017. "Calls of the Wild? 'Fake' Sound Effects and Cinematic Realism in BBC David Attenborough Nature Documentaries." *The Soundtrack (Bristol)*, 10(1), pp. 59–77. https://doi.org/10.1386/ts.10.1.59_1.

Conn, S. 2014. *Americans Against the City: Anti-urbanism in the Twentieth Century.* Oxford: Oxford University Press. Kindle Edition.

Crary, J. 2013. *24/7: Terminal Capitalism and the Ends of Sleep.* London: Verso.

Cronon, W. 1995. "The Trouble with Wilderness; or, Getting Back to the Wrong Nature." In: Cronon, W. ed. *Uncommon Ground: Rethinking the Human Place in Nature.* New York: W. W. Norton & Co., pp. 69–90.

Damm, C. 2016. "Enfolded by the Long Winter's Night." In: Dowd, M. and Hensey, R. eds. *Archeology of Darkness.* Oxford: Oxbow Books. Kindle Edition, pp. 107–116.

The Dark: Nature's Nighttime World. 2012. [Film] Directed by Joe Loncraine. United Kingdom: BBC.

Decolonizing Light. n.d. Available at: https://decolonizinglight.com/#:~:text=The%20Decolonizing%20Light%20project%20explores,relation%20of%20science%20and%20colonialism [Accessed 23 September 2024].

DeLoughrey, E. 2014. "Satellite Planetarity and the Ends of the Earth." *Public Culture,* 26(2), pp. 257–280.

Demars, S.E. 1990. "Romanticism and American National Parks." *Journal of Cultural Geography,* 11(1), pp. 17–24.

Denevan, W.M. 1992. "The Pristine Myth: The Landscape of the Americas in 1492." *Annals of the Association of American Geographers,* 82(3), pp. 369–385.

Dewey, J. 1999. *Individualism, Old and New.* Amherst, NY: Prometheus.

Dillon, G.L. 2012. *Walking the Clouds: An Anthology of Indigenous Science Fiction.* Tucson: University of Arizona Press.

Diogo, M.P., Louro, I. and Scarso, D. 2017. "UNCANNY NATURE: Why the Concept of Anthropocene Is Relevant for Historians of Technology." *Icon,* 23, pp. 25–35.

Donahue, M.Z. 2016. "80 Percent of Americans Can't See the Milky Way Anymore." *National Geographic,* June. Available at: https://www.nationalgeographic.com/science/article/milky-wayspacescience#:~:text=But%20a%20new%20atlas%20of,Way%20has%20become%20virtually%20invisible [Accessed 30 January 2023].

Douglas, M. 2002. *Purity and Danger: An Analysis of Concept of Pollution and Taboo.* Abingdon: Routledge.

Driskill, Q. 2016. *Asegi Stories: Cherokee Queer and Two-Spirit Memory.* Tucson: University of Arizona Press.

Dunn, N. 2021. *Dark Matters: A Manifesto for the Nocturnal City.* Winchester, UK: Zero. Kindle Edition.

Dunn, N. and Edensor, T. 2021. *Rethinking Darkness: Cultures, Histories, Practices.* New York: Routledge. Kindle Edition.

Dunnett, O. 2015. "Contested Landscapes: The Moral Geographies of Light Pollution in Britain." *Cultural Geographies,* 22(4), pp. 619–636.

Earth at Night in Color. 2020. [Film] Directed by Tom Hugh-Jones. United Kingdom: Offspring Films.

EarthSky Voices. 2019. "US astronomers speak on SpaceX Starlink satellites," 9 June. Available at: https://earthsky.org/human-world/aas-statement-spacex-starlink-satellites/ [Accessed 5 June 2024].

Easterling, K. 2014. *Extrastatecraft: The Power of Infrastructure Space.* London: Verso.

Edensor, T. 2014. "The Rich Potentialities of Light Festivals". In: Meier, J., Hasenöhrl, U., Krause, K., & Pottharst, M. (eds.) *Urban lighting, light pollution and society.* New York: Routledge, pp. 85–98.

Edensor, T. 2015a. "The Gloomy City: Rethinking the Relationship between Light and Dark." *Urban Studies,* 52(3), pp. 422–438. https://doi.org/10.1177/0042098013504009

Edensor, T. 2015b. "Light Design and Atmosphere." *Visual Communication,* 14(3), pp. 331–350. https://doi.org/10.1177/1470357215579975

Edensor, T. 2017. *From Light to Dark: Daylight, Illumination, and Gloom.* Minneapolis: University of Minnesota Press.

Eklöf, J. 2023. *The Darkness Manifesto Why the World Needs the Night.* Translated by Elizabeth DeNoma. Dublin: Vintage. Kindle Edition.

Elcott, N.M. 2016. *Artificial Darkness: An Obscure History of Modern Art and Media.* Chicago: University of Chicago Press.

Emerson, R.W. 2019. *Nature and Other Essays.* Mineola, NY: Dover Publications. Kindle Edition.

Escario-Sierra, F., Alvarez-Alonso, G., Mosene-Fierro, J.A. and Sanagustin-Fons, V. 2022. "Sustainable Tourism, Social and Institutional Innovation – The Paradox of Dark Sky in Astrotourism." *Sustainability*, 14(11), pp. 1–20.

Farajirad, A. and Beiki, P. 2015. "Codification of Appropriate Strategies to Astronomical Tourism Development." (Seghaleh, South of Khorasan).

Fayos-solà, E. et al.2014. "Astrotourism: No Requiem for Meaningful Travel." *PASOS Revista de Turismo y Patrimonio Cultural*, 12, pp. 663–671.

Fernando, M. 2022. "Uncanny Ecologies: More-than-Natural, More-than-Human, More-than-Secular." *Comparative Studies of South Asia, Africa, and the Middle East*, 42(3), pp. 568–583. https://doi.org/10.1215/1089201X-10148233.

Fernholz, T. 2018. *Rocket Billionaires: Elon Musk, Jeff Bezos, and the New Space Race.* Boston: Houghton Mifflin Harcourt.

Ferreira, B. 2021. "SpaceX's Satellite Megaconstellations Are Astrocolonialism, Indigenous Advocates Say," *MotherBoard*, 5 October. Available at: https://www.vice.com/en/article/k78mnz/spacexs-satellite-megaconstellations-are-astrocolonialism-indigenous-advocates-say [Accessed 27 September 2024].

Fisher, M. 2016. *The Weird and the Eerie.* 3rd Edition. London: Repeater Books. Kindle Edition.

Florida, R. 2017. *The New Urban Crisis: How Our Cities Are Increasing Inequality, Deepening Segregation, and Failing the Middle Class-and What We Can Do About It.* New York: Basic Books.

Florida, R. 2019. *The Rise of the Creative Class.* New York: Basic Books.

Freud, S. 1955. "The "Uncanny" [1919]." In: Strachey, J., Freud, A., Strachey, A., & Tyson, A. (eds.) *The Complete Psychological Works.* Vol. XVII. London: Hogarth Press, pp. 217–256.

Gallaway, T. 2010. "On Light Pollution, Passive Pleasures, and the Instrumental Value of Beauty." *Journal of Economic Issues*, 44(1), pp. 71–88.

Ghosh, A. 2016. *The Great Derangement: Climate Change and the Unthinkable.* Chicago: The University of Chicago Press. Kindle Edition.

Giblett, R.J. 2019. *Environmental Humanities and the Uncanny: Ecoculture, Literature and Religion.* Abingdon: Routledge.

Giordano, E. and Ong, C.E. 2017. "Light Festivals, Policy Mobilities and Urban Tourism." *Tourism Geographies*, 19(5), pp. 699–716.

Greene, S. 2020. "'Night on Earth' Review: Netflix's Nocturnal Nature Doc Is Built Like a Dispatch from Another Planet." *IndieWire.* Available at: https://www.indiewire.com/criticism/shows/night-on-earth-netflix-review-nature-series-1202206848/ [Accessed 4 December 2024].

Griffiths, A. 2008. *Shivers Down Your Spine: Cinema, Museums, and the Immersive View.* 1st Edition. New York: Columbia University Press. Kindle Edition.

Grusin, R.A. 2004. *Culture, Technology, and the Creation of America's National Parks.* Vol. 137. Cambridge, UK: Cambridge University Press.

Gorman, A. 2019. *Dr Space Junk Vs The Universe: Archaeology and the Future.* Cambridge: MIT Press.

Guo, K., Fan, A., Lehto, X. and Day, J. 2023. "Immersive Digital Tourism: The Role of Multisensory Cues in Digital Museum Experiences." *Journal of Hospitality & Tourism Research*, 47(6), pp. 1017–1039.

Gwiazdzinski, L. 2016. "Urban Night Introduction: The Urban Night: A Space Time for Innovation and Sustainable Development." *Articulo – Journal of Urban Research*, n°11.

Gwiazdzinski, L. and Straw, W. 2018. "Nights and Mountains. Preliminary Explorations of a Double Frontier."*Journal of Alpine Research/Revue de géographie alpine*, 106(1).

Hamacher, D. 2023. *The First Astronomers: How Indigenous Elders Read the Stars.* Crows Nest, Australia: Allen & Unwin. Kindle Edition.

Han, B.C. 2017. *The Scent of Time: A Philosophical Essay on the Art of Lingering.* New York: Polity. Kindle Edition.

Harman, G. 2010. *Towards Speculative Realism: Essays and Lectures.* Winchester, UK: Zero Books. Kindle Edition.

Hay, J. 2020. "The Invention of Air Space, Outer Space, and Cyberspace." In: Parks, L. and Schwoch, J., ed. *Down to Earth.* Ithaca, NY: Rutgers University Press, pp. 19–41.

Hays, P.L. 2015. "Spacepower Theory." In: *Handbook of Space Security.* New York: Springer, pp. 57–79.

Hensey, R. 2016. "Past Dark: A Short Introduction to the Human Relationships with Darkness Over Time." In Dowd, M. and Hensey, R., eds. *Archeology of Darkness.* Oxford: Oxbow Books, pp. 1–10. Kindle Edition.

Holt, D. 2012. "Transformation of Unsustainable Markets Constructing Sustainable Consumption: From Ethical Values." *The ANNALS of the American Academy of Political and Social Science*, 644, pp. 236–255.

Horak, J.C. 2006. "Wildlife Documentaries: From Classical Forms to Reality TV." *Film History: An International Journal*, 18(4), pp. 454–475.

Ingold, T. 2021. *The Perception of the Environment: Essays on Livelihood, Dwelling and Skill.* New edition. London: Routledge.

Isenstadt, S. 2018. *Electric Light: An Architectural History.* Cambridge, MA: The MIT Press. https://doi.org/10.7551/mitpress/11305.001.0001.

Janowitz, A. 2005. "What a Rich Fund of Images Is Treasured up Here: Poetic Commonplaces of the Sublime Universe." *Studies in Romanticism*, 44(4), pp. 469–492.

Justice, D.H. 2008. "Fear of a Changeling Moon: A Rather Queer Tale from a Cherokee Hillbilly." In: Taylor, D.H. ed. *Me Sexy: An Exploration of Native Sex and Sexuality.* Madeiera Park, B.C.: Douglas & McIntyre.

Justice, D.H. 2017. "Indigenous Wonderworks and the Settler-Colonial Imaginary." *Apex Magazine*, 10 August. Available at: https://apex-magazine.com/nonfiction/indigenous-wonderworks-and-the-settler-colonial-imaginary/ [Accessed 27 September 2024].

Justice, D.H. 2018. *Why Indigenous Literatures Matter.* Waterloo: Wilfrid Laurier University Press. Kindle Edition.

Kessler, E.A. 2012. *Picturing the Cosmos: Hubble Space Telescope Images and the Astronomical Sublime.* Minneapolis: University of Minnesota Press.

Klinkrad, H. 2006. *Space Debris Models and Risk Analysis.* Berlin: Springer.

Knight, K.B. 2015. "The Work of iamamiwhoami in the Age of Networked Transmission." *The Projector: A Journal on Film, Media, and Culture*, 15(1), Winter, pp. 8–46.

Koslofsky, C. 2011. *Evening's Empire: A History of the Night in Early Modern Europe.* Cambridge: Cambridge University Press. Kindle Edition.

Kukiiyaut, M. 1989. "Spirits of the Night." Available at: https://nativecanadianarts.com/gallery/spirits-of-the-night/ [Accessed 13 May 2024].

Kukiiyaut, M. 2024. "Spirits of the Night." DaVic Gallery. Available at: https://nativecanadianarts.com/gallery/spirits-of-the-night/ [Accessed 20 June 2024].

Landry, C. 2012. *The Art of City Making.* London: Routledge.

Lang, F. 1927. Director. *Metropolis*, Paramount Pictures.

Latour, B. 2012. "Love Your Monsters: Why We Must Care for Our Technologies As We Do Our Children." *The Breakthrough Institute.* Available at: https://thebreakthrough.org/journal/issue-2/love-your-monsters.

Lee, L.H. 2022. *Worlds Unbound: The Art of teamLab.* 1st Edition. Bristol, England: Intellect Ltd.

Levi-Straus, Claude. 2003. *Myth and Meaning.* New York: Taylor & Francis.

Longcore, T. and Rich, C. 2013. *Ecological Consequences of Artificial Night Lighting.* Washington, D.C.: Island Press.

Lopez, I. 2024. *True Detective: Night Country.* New York: HBO Films.

Lorde, A. 2024. "Uses of the Erotic: The Erotic as Power." Available at: https://www.centraleurasia.org/wp-content/uploads/2023/02/audre_lorde_cool-beans.pdf [Accessed 3 October 2024].

Lorimer, H. 2005. "Cultural Geography: The Busyness of Being 'More-Than-Representational.'" *Progress in Human Geography*, 29, pp. 83–94.

Louson, E. 2021. "Performing Authenticity: The Making-of Documentary in Wildlife Film's Blue-chip Renaissance." *People and Nature (Hoboken, N.J.)*, 3(6), pp. 1147–1159.

Lyle, D. 1995. "Pibloktoq (Arctic Hysteria): A Construction of European-Inuit Relations?" *Arctic Anthropology*, 32(2), pp. 1–42.

MacDiarind, Campbell. 2024. "Ottawa's First 'night mayor' Is on a Mission to Shed City's Boring Reputation." *The Guardian*, 9, July, 2024, https://www.theguardian.com/world/article/2024/jul/09/ottawa-canada-night-mayor.

Martin, K. 2012. *Stories in a New Skin: Approaches to Inuit Literature.* Winnipeg: University of Manitoba Press. Kindle Edition.

Massey, D. 1991. "A Global Sense of Place." *Marxism Today*, 35(6), pp. 24–29.

Massey, D. 1994. *Space, Place, and Gender.* Minneapolis: University of Minnesota Press.

McCray, P. 2021. *Keep Watching the Skies! The Story of Operation Moonwatch and the Dawn of the Space Age.* Princeton: Princeton University Press. Kindle Edition.

Melbin, M. 1987. *Night as Frontier: Colonizing World After Dark.* New York: Free Press.

Mirzoeff, N. 2011. "The Right to Look." *Critical Inquiry*, 37(3), pp. 473–96.

Mirzoeff, N. 2014. "Visualizing the Anthropocene." *Public Culture*, 26(2), pp. 213–32.

Mitchell, D. and Gallaway, T. 2019. "Dark Sky Tourism: Economic Impacts on the Colorado Plateau Economy, USA." *Tourism Review*, 74(4), pp. 930–942.

Mitman, G. 2009. *Reel Nature: America's Romance with Wildlife on Film.* Seattle: University of Washington Press.

Mortillaro, N. 2023. "Goodbye, Dark Sky. The Stars Are Rapidly Disappearing from Our Night Sky." *CBC News*, 19 January. Available at: https://www.cbc.ca/news/science/light-pollution-increasing-1.6719034.

Morton, T. 2010. "Guest Column: Queer Ecology." *PMLA: Publications of the Modern Language Association of America*, 125(2), pp. 273–82.

Morton, T. 2013. *Hyperobjects: Philosophy and Ecology after the End of the World.* Minneapolis: University of Minnesota Press.

Morton, T. 2021. *Hyposubjects: On Becoming Human.* London: Open Humanities Press.

Muir, J. 2020. *Our National Parks.* New York: HarperCollins:. Kindle Edition.

"Nalujuit: Intangible Cultural Heritage." 2024. Available at: https://www.mun.ca/ich/search-ich-collections/hearts-content/christmas-traditions/nalujuit/ [Accessed 6 June 2024].

Nelson, M. 2017. "Getting Dirty: The Eco-Eroticism of Women in Indigenous Oral Literatures." In Barker, J. ed. *Critically Sovereign: Indigenous Gender, Sexuality, and Feminist Studies.* Durham: Duke University Press.

Neumann, M. 1999. *On the Rim: Looking for the Grand Canyon.* Minnesota: University of Minnesota Press. Kindle Edition.

Night of the Lion. Washinton, D.C.: *National Geographic Channel.*

Night on Earth. 2020. *Netflix Studios.* Burbank, California.

Night on Earth: Shot in the Dark. 2020. *Netflix Studios.* Burbank, California.

Palmer, B.D. 2000. *Cultures of Darkness: Night Travels in the Histories of Transgression.* New York, NY: Monthly Review Press.

Parks, L. 2005. *Cultures in Orbit.* Durham, NC: Duke University Press.

Pasternak, A. and Thompson, N. 2012. "Forward." In: Paglen, T., ed. *The Last Pictures.* Oakland, California: University of California Press., pp. xxi–ix.

Patin, T. 2012. *Observation Points: The Visual Poetics of National Parks.* Minnesota: University of Minnesota Press.

Pay, M.A. 2019. "Anna Tsing, Heather Swanson, Elaine Gan, and Nils Bubandt (Eds), Arts of Living on a Damaged Planet: Ghosts and Monsters of the Anthropocene." *Environmental Values*, 28(5), pp. 624–26.

Peterschmidt, D. 2020. "Relearning the Star Stories of Indigenous Peoples." *Science Friday*, 9 June. Available at: https://www.sciencefriday.com/articles/indigenous-peoples-astronomy/ [Accessed 27 September 2024].

Petrovics, N. and Seijas, A. 2020. "Nighttime Governance in Times of COVID-19." In *Global Nighttime Recovery Plan.* ViveLabs. Available at: https://www.mcgill.ca/centre-montreal/files/centre-montreal/ch5_nighttime_governance_gnrp.pdf.

Prelli, L.J. 2006. "Rhetorics of Display: An Introduction." In: Prelli, L, ed. *Rhetorics of Display.* Columbia, SC: University of South Carolina Press, pp. 1–40.

Richling, B. 1980. "Images of the 'Heathen' in Northern Labrador." *Études Inuit Studies*, 4(1/2), pp. 233–242.

Rubenstein, M.J. 2008. *Strange Wonder: The Closure of Metaphysics and the Opening of Awe.* New York: Columbia University Press. Kindle Edition.

Sagan, C. 2011. *Pale Blue Dot: A Vision of the Human Future in Space.* New York: Ballatine Books. Kindle Edition.

Schlör, J. 1998. *Nights in the Big City: Paris, Berlin, London 1840–1930.* London: Reaktion Books.

Schwartz, N.A. 2022. *Orbital Debris and Kinetic Anti-Satellite Concerns: How a "Kessler Syndrome" Threatens U.S. Use of Space Assets.* Alexandia, Virginia: Institute for Defense Analyses.

Scott, K.D. 2003. "Popularizing Science and Nature Programming: The Role of 'Spectacle' in Contemporary Wildlife Documentary." *Journal of Popular Film and Television*, 31(1), pp. 29–35. https://doi.org/10.1080/01956050309602866.

Shaviro, S. 2014. *The Universe of Things: On Speculative Realism.* Minneapolis: University of Minnesota Press. Kindle Edition.

Shaw, R. 2014. "Controlling Darkness: Self, Dark and the Domestic Night." *Cultural Geographies*, 22(4), pp. 585–600.

Smith, S.M. and Sliwinski, S. 2017. *Photography and the Optical Unconscious.* Durham: Duke University Press.

Silver, D.A. and Hickey, G.M. 2020. "Managing Light Pollution through Dark Sky Areas: Learning from the World's First Dark Sky Preserve." *Journal of Environmental Planning and Management*, 63(14), pp. 2627–2645.

Straw, W. 2005. "Unity and Division in the Urban Night." In *Coexisting in Urban Nights: From the Meanings of Shadow to the Regulations of Ordinary Night Investment.* Paris, Harmattan.

Straw, W. 2015. "Media and the Urban Night." *Articulo*, 11. https://doi.org/10.4000/articulo.3098.

Straw, W. 2018. "Unity and Division in the Urban Night." In: Guerin, F. ed. *Coexisting in Urban Nights.* Paris: Harmattan.

Sumartojo, S. 2015. "On Atmosphere and Darkness at Australia''s Anzac Day Dawn Service." *Visual Communication*, 14(3), pp. 267–88.

Tallas, A., dir. 2014. *Life on Us.* Melbourne, Screen Australia.

Tagaq, T. 2019. *Split Tooth.* New York: Harper Collins. Kindle Edition.

Tennyson, A.L. . "God and the Universe." Simple Poetry, https://www.simple-poetry.com/poems/god-and-the-universe-19903248833.

Toposophy. "The 24/7 Revolution: How Cities Are Transforming Their Night Economies." https://toposhopy.cdn.prismic.io/toposhopy/65b0d01a615e73009ec3dfd6_The247revolution_pdf.pdf [Accessed 9 April 2025].

Urry, J. 1994. "Time, Leisure and Social Identity." *Time & Society*, 3(2), pp. 131–149.

Van Doren, B.M., Horton, K.G., Dokter, A.M., Klinck, H., Elbin, S.B. and Farnsworth, A. 2017. "High-Intensity Urban Light Installation Dramatically Alters Nocturnal Bird Migration." *Proceedings of the National Academy of Sciences – PNAS*, 114(42), pp. 11175–11180. https://doi.org/10.1073/pnas.1708574114.

Van Dyke, H. 2005. *The Poems of Henry Van Dyke.* Washington, D.C.: The Gutenberg Project.

Van Dyke, H. 2005. "Wordless Worship." *The Project Gutenberg eBook of The Poems of Henry van Dyke.* Project Gutenberg. https://www.poetryfoundation.org/poem.

van Liempt, I., van Aalst, I. and Schwanen, T. 2015. "Introduction: Geographies of the Urban Night." *Urban Studies (Edinburgh, Scotland)*, 52(3), pp. 407–21. https://doi.org/10.1177/0042098014552933.

Venkatesan, A., Lowenthal, J. and Prem, P. 2020. "The Impact of Satellite Constellations on Space as an Ancestral Global Commons." *Nature Astronomy*, 4, pp. 1043–1048.

Viney, W. 2015. *Waste: A Philosophy of Things.* London: Bloomsbury Publishing. Kindle Edition.

Virilio, P. 2000. *A Landscape of Events.* Trans. Julie Rose. Cambridge: MIT Press.

Walker, C. et al. 2020. "Satellite Constellations 1 Workshop Report." Available at: https://aas.org/sites/default/files/2020-08/SATCON1-Report.pdf.

Ward, J. 2001. *Weimar Surfaces: Urban Visual Culture in 1920s Germany.* Oakland, California: University of California Press. Kindle Edition.

Ward, S. 2005. *Selling Places: The Marketing and Promotion of Towns and Cities 1850–2000.* London: Taylor & Francis.

Weaver, D. 2011. "Celestial Ecotourism: New Horizons in Nature-Based Tourism." *Journal of Ecotourism*, 10(1), pp. 38–45.

Williams, J. 2020. *Nalujuk Night.* Ottawa: National Film Board of Canada.

Witze, A. 2018. "The Quest to Conquer Earth's Space Junk Problem." *Nature (London)*, 561(7721), pp. 24–26. https://doi.org/10.1038/d41586-018-06170-1.

Woods, M. 2005. *Rural Geography: Processes, Responses and Experiences in Rural Restructuring.* London: Sage Publications.

Woods, M. 2010. *Rural.* London: Routledge.

Young, N. 2012. "Uses of the Erotic for Teaching Queer Studies." *Women's Studies Quarterly*, 40(3/4), pp. 301–305.

Zallen, J. 2019. *American Lucifers: The Dark History of Artificial Light, 1750–1865.* Chapel Hill: University of North Carolina Press.

INDEX

www.ingramcontent.com/pod-product-compliance
Lightning Source LLC
LaVergne TN
LVHW091001080826
845145LV00003B/1079

* 9 7 8 1 8 0 1 3 6 0 5 5 5 *